Moving Forth - Part 1 – 8

A Minimal TTL Processor

B.Y.O. Assembler

Selected Articles

by

Brad Rodriguez

The current Forth Bookshelf can be found at
https://www.amazon.co.uk/Juergen-Pintaske/e/B00N8HVEZM

1 Charles Moore - Forth - The Early Years: Background information about the beginnings of this Computer Language
2 Charles Moore - Programming A Problem Oriented Language: Forth - how the internals work
3 Leo Brodie - Starting Forth -The Classic
4 Leo Wong – Juergen Pintaske – Stephen Pelc FORTH LITE TUTORIAL: Code tested with free MPE VFX Forth, SwiftForth and Gforth or else
5 Juergen Pintaske – A START WITH FORTH - Bits to Bites Collection – 12 Words to start, then 35 Words, Javascript Forth on the Web, more
6 Stephen Pelc - Programming Forth: Version July 2016
7 Brad Rodriguez - Moving Forth / TTL CPU / B.Y.O. Assembler
8 Tim Hentlass - Real Time Forth

9 Chen-Hanson Ting - Footsteps In An Empty Valley issue 3
10 Chen-Hanson Ting - Zen and the Forth Language: EFORTH for the MSP430G2552 from Texas Instruments
11 Chen-Hanson Ting - eForth and Zen - 3rd Edition 2017: with 32-bit 86eForth v5.2 for Visual Studio 2015
12 Chen-Hanson Ting - eForth Overview
13 Chen-Hanson Ting - FIG-Forth Manual Document /Test in 1802 IP
14 Chen-Hanson Ting - EP32 RISC Processor IP: Description and Implementation into FPGA – ASIC tested by NASA
15 Chen-Hanson Ting – Irriducible Complexity

16 Burkhard Kainka - Learning Programming with MyCo: Learning Programming easily - independent of a PC (Forth code to follow soon)
17 Burkhard Kainka - BBC Micro:bit: Tests Tricks Secrets Code, Additional MicroBit information when running the Mecrisp Package
18 Burkhard Kainka – Thomas Baum – Web Programming ATYTINY13

Introduction

In 2018 we celebrate ***50 Years of Forth***. And when I looked for a new eBook project, I realized that one area is not very well covered:

How do the Forth internals work?

How can you build a Minimal Processor executing Forth directly?

How do you write an Assembler in Forth?

When I looked around for some documentation, I remembered Brad's excellent series of articles again. They seemed to fit very well together.

I contacted Brad and asked for permission to publish them and add them to the Forth Bookshelf I had started 5 years ago.

He liked the idea, so I started editing and formatting. I did not change any of the original material. The only part I added was an appendix, where I re-did some of the pictures in Excel, so I could understand them better.

And as in many cases, additional material will be made available on the www.Forth-eV.de Wiki, we will start with the appendix added there to download and edit locally, and add more that we might come up with.

There are many references and links as part of the articles – a good source to search for additional information for interested parties.

This is not new material – actually exactly 25 years old (half the Forth age) - but is still the best material I could find for this project to understand the Forth Internals better - covering Software and Hardware. And more importantly: the Forth structure is stable and has not changed that much. Probably one reason why no new material has been done.

I have to thank Brad Rodriguez for the copyright to publish this documentation.

Enjoy reading and any feedback please send to epldfpga@aol.com.

There is another eBook which covers similar aspects: Chen-Hanson Ting's eForth Overview at https://www.amazon.co.uk/eForth-Overview-C-H-Ting-ebook/dp/B01LR47JME/ref=asap_bc?ie=UTF8

I recently started converting the eBooks to print books, so Charles Moore, the inventor of Forth, has the chance at EuroForth 2018 in September in Scotland at the river of Forth, to hold his first book **Programming a Problem-Oriented Language** in his hand, plus some more.

In print now – and more to come, just check on amazon:
2 **Charles Moore** - Programming A Problem Oriented Language: Forth
4 **Leo Wong – Juergen Pintaske – Stephen Pelc** FORTH LITE TUTORIAL:
5 **Juergen Pintaske – A START WITH FORTH** - Bits to Bites Collection
6 **Stephen Pelc** - Programming Forth: Version July 2016
7 **Brad Rodriguez** - Moving Forth / TTL CPU / B.Y.O. Assembler

And if you are interested in finding out, which of those are of interest to the amazon community, check it yourself in the actual top 100 Bestseller list in Compiler Design:
https://www.amazon.com/gp/bestsellers/books/3970/ref=pd_zg_hrsr_b_1_5_last#5

Juergen Pintaske, ExMark, 11 August 2018

Contents:

Book_Brad_Rodriguez-Forth_v15a

Pictures in this eBook:

Chapter 1

Chapter 3

Chapter 6

Chapter 7

A Minimal TTL Processor

MOVING FORTH by Brad Rodriguez

Part 1: Design Decisions in the Forth Kernel

Part 1: Design Decisions in the Forth Kernel

This article first appeared in **The Computer Journal** #59 (January/February 1993).

1.1 INTRODUCTION

Everyone in the Forth community talks about how easy it is to port Forth to a new CPU. But like many "easy" and "obvious" tasks, not much is written on how to do it! So, when Bill Kibler suggested this topic for an article, I decided to break with the great oral tradition of Forthwrights, and document the process in black and white.

Over the course of these articles I will develop Forths for the 6809, 8051, and Z80. I'm doing the 6809 to illustrate an easy and conventional Forth model; plus, I've already published a 6809 assembler [ROD91,ROD92], and I'll be needing a 6809 Forth for future TCJ projects. I'm doing the 8051 Forth for a University project, but it also illustrates some rather different design decisions. The Z80 Forth is for all the CP/M readers of TCJ, and for some friends with TRS-80s gathering dust.

1.2 THE ESSENTIAL HARDWARE

You must choose a CPU. I will not delve into the merits of one CPU over another for Forth, since a CPU choice is usually forced upon you by other considerations. Besides, the object of this article is to show how to move Forth to any CPU.

You can expect the usual 16-bit Forth kernel (see below) to occupy about 8K bytes of program space. For a full kernel that can compile Forth definitions, you should allow a minimum of 1K byte of RAM. To use Forth's block-management system for disk storage, you should add 3 Kbytes or more for buffers. For a 32-bit Forth model, double these numbers.

These are the minimums to get a Forth kernel up and running. To run an application on your hardware, you should increase PROM and RAM sizes to suit.

1.3 16 OR 32 BIT?

The word size used by Forth is not necessarily the same as that of the CPU. The smallest practical Forth is a 16-bit model; i.e., one which uses 16-bit integers and 16-bit addresses. The Forth community calls this the "cell" size, since "word" refers to a Forth definition.

8-bit CPUs almost invariably support 16-bit Forths. This usually requires explicit coding of double-byte arithmetic, although some 8-bit CPUs do have a few 16-bit operations.

16-bit CPUs commonly run 16-bit Forths, although the same double- precision techniques can be used to write a 32-bit Forth on a 16- bit CPU. At least one 32-bit Forth has been written for the 8086/8088.

32-bit CPUs normally run 32-bit Forths. A smaller Forth model rarely saves code length or processor time. However, I know of at least one 16-bit Forth written for the 68000. This does shrink application code size by a factor of two, since high-level Forth definitions become a string of 16-bit addresses rather than a string of 32-bit addresses. (This will become evident shortly.) Most 68000s, though, have plenty of RAM.

All of the examples described in this article are 16-bit Forths running on 8-bit CPUs.

1.4 THE THREADING TECHNIQUE

"Threaded code" is the hallmark of Forth. A Forth "thread" is just a list of addresses of routines to be executed. You can think of this as a list of subroutine calls, with the CALL instructions removed. Over the years many threading variations have been devised, and which one is best depends upon the CPU and the application. To make a decision, you need to understand how they work, and their tradeoffs.

1.5 Indirect Threaded Code (ITC)

This is the classical Forth threading technique, used in fig- Forth and F83, and described in most books on Forth. All the other threading schemes are "improvements" on this, so you need to understand ITC to appreciate the others.
Let's look at the definition of a Forth word SQUARE:

: SQUARE DUP * ;

In a typical ITC Forth this would appear in memory as shown in Figure 1. (The header will be discussed in a future article; it holds housekeeping information used for compilation, and isn't involved in threading.)

FIGURE 1. INDIRECT THREADED CODE

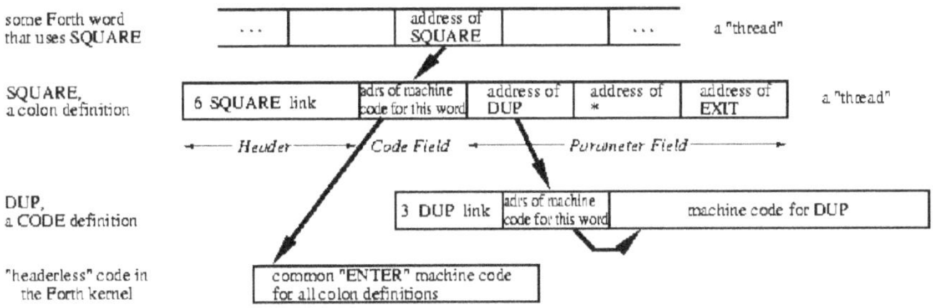

Assume SQUARE is encountered while executing some other Forth word. Forth's Interpreter Pointer (IP) will be pointing to a cell in memory -- contained within that "other" word -- which contains the address of the word SQUARE. (To be precise, that cell contains the address of SQUARE's Code Field.) The interpreter fetches that address, and then uses it to fetch the contents of SQUARE's Code Field. These contents are yet another address -- the address of a machine language subroutine which performs the word SQUARE. In pseudo-code, this is:

(IP) -> W	**fetch memory pointed by IP into "W" register ...W now holds address of the Code Field**
IP+2 -> IP	**advance IP, just like a program counter (assuming 2-byte addresses in the thread)**
(W) -> X	**fetch memory pointed by W into "X" register ...X now holds address of the machine code**
JP (X)	**jump to the address in the X register**

This illustrates an important but rarely-elucidated principle: the address of the Forth word just entered is kept in W. CODE words don't need this information, but all other kinds of Forth words do.

If SQUARE were written in machine code, this would be the end of the story: that bit of machine code would be executed, and then jump back to the Forth interpreter -- which, since IP was incremented, is pointing to the next word to be executed. This is why the Forth interpreter is usually called NEXT.

But, SQUARE is a high-level "colon" definition -- it holds a "thread", a list of addresses. In order to perform this definition, the Forth interpreter must be re-started at a new location: the Parameter Field of SQUARE. Of course, the interpreter's old location must be saved, to resume the "other" Forth word once SQUARE is finished. This is just like a subroutine call! The machine language action of SQUARE is simply to push the old IP, set IP to a new location, run the interpreter, and when SQUARE is done pop the IP. (As you can see, the IP is the "program counter" of high-level Forth.) This is called DOCOLON or ENTER in various Forths:

	PUSH IP	**onto the "return address stack"**
	W+2 -> IP	**W still points to the Code Field, so W+2 is the address of the Body! (Assuming a 2-byte address -- other Forths may be different.)**
	JUMP	**to interpreter ("NEXT")**

This identical code fragment is used by all high-level (i.e., threaded) Forth definitions! That's why a pointer to this code fragment, not the fragment itself, is included in the Forth definition. Over hundreds of definitions, the savings add up! And this is why it's called Indirect threading.

The "return from subroutine" is the word EXIT, which gets compiled when Forth sees ';'. (Some Forths call it ;S instead of EXIT.) EXIT just executes a machine language routine which does the following:

	POP IP	**from the "return address stack"**
	JUMP	**to interpreter**

Walk through a couple of nested Forth definitions, just to assure yourself that this works.

Note the characteristics of ITC: every Forth word has a one-cell Code Field. Colon definitions compile one cell for each word used in the definition. And the Forth interpreter must actually perform a double indirection to get the address of the next machine code to run (first through IP, then through W).

ITC is neither the smallest nor the fastest threading technique. It may be the simplest; although DTC (described next) is really no more complex. So why are so many Forths indirect-threaded? Mainly because previous Forths, used as models, were indirect-threaded. These days, DTC is becoming more popular.

So when should ITC be used? Of the various techniques, ITC produces the cleanest and most elegant definitions -- nothing but addresses. If you're attuned to such considerations, ITC may appeal to you. If your code fiddles around with the insides of definitions, the simplicity and uniformity of the ITC representation may enhance portability. ITC is the classical Forth model, so it may be preferred for education. Finally, on CPUs lacking a subroutine call instruction -- such as the 1802 -- ITC is often more efficient than DTC.

1.6 Direct Threaded Code (DTC)

Direct Threaded Code differs from ITC in only one respect: instead of the Code Field containing the address of some machine code, the Code Field contains actual machine code itself.

I'm not saying that the complete code for ENTER is contained in each and every colon definition! In "high-level" Forth words, the Code Field will contain a subroutine call, as shown in Figure 2. Colon definitions, for instance, will contain a call to the ENTER routine.

FIGURE 2. DIRECT THREADED CODE

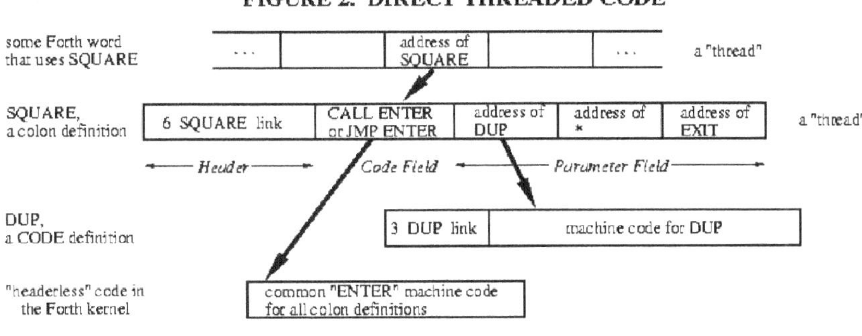

The NEXT pseudo-code for direct threading is simply:

(IP) -> W	**fetch memory pointed by IP into "W" register**
IP+2 -> IP	**advance IP (assuming 2-byte addresses)**
JP (W)	**jump to the address in the W register**

This gains speed: the interpreter now performs only a single indirection. On the Z80 this reduces the NEXT routine -- the most-used code fragment in the Forth kernel -- from eleven instructions to seven!

This costs space: every high-level definition in a Z80 Forth (for example) is now one byte longer, since a 2-byte address has been replaced by a 3-byte call. But this is not universally true. A 32-bit 68000 Forth may replace a 4-byte address with a 4-byte BSR instruction, for no net loss. And on the Zilog Super8, which has machine instructions for DTC Forth, the 2-byte address is replaced by a 1-byte ENTER instruction, making a DTC Forth smaller on the Super8!

Of course, DTC CODE definitions are two bytes shorter, since they no longer need a pointer at all!

I used to think that high-level definitions in DTC Forths required the use of a subroutine call in the Code Field. Frank Sergeant's Pygmy Forth [SER90] demonstrates that a simple jump can be used just as easily, and will usually be faster.

Guy Kelly has compiled a superb review of Forth implementations for the IBM PC [KEL92], which I strongly recommend to all Forth kernel writers. Of the 19 Forths he studied, 10 used DTC, 7 used ITC, and 2 used subroutine threading (discussed next). I recommend the use of Direct-Threaded Code over Indirect-Threaded Code for all new Forth kernels.

1.7 Jump to NEXT, or code it in-line?

The Forth inner interpreter, NEXT, is a common routine to all CODE definitions. You might keep just one copy of this common routine, and have all CODE words jump to it. (Note that you Jump to NEXT; a subroutine Call is not necessary.)

However, the speed of NEXT is crucial to the speed of the entire Forth system. Also, on many CPUs, the NEXT routine is quite short; often only two or three instructions. So it may be preferable to code NEXT in-line, wherever it is used. This is frequently done by making NEXT an assembler macro.

This is a simple speed vs. space decision: in-line NEXT is always faster, but almost always larger. The total size increase is the number of extra bytes required for in-line expansion, times the number of CODE words in the system. Sometimes there's no tradeoff at all: in a 6809 DTC Forth, an in-line NEXT is shorter than a Jump instruction!

1.8 Subroutine Threaded Code (STC)

A high-level Forth definition is nothing but a list of subroutines to be executed. You don't need interpreters to accomplish this; you can get the same effect by simply stringing a list of subroutine calls together:

SQUARE: CALL DUP	
CALL *	; or a suitable alphanumeric name
RET	

See Figure 3. This representation of Forth words has been used as a starting point to explain Forth threading techniques to assembly language programmers [KOG82].

FIGURE 3. SUBROUTINE THREADED CODE

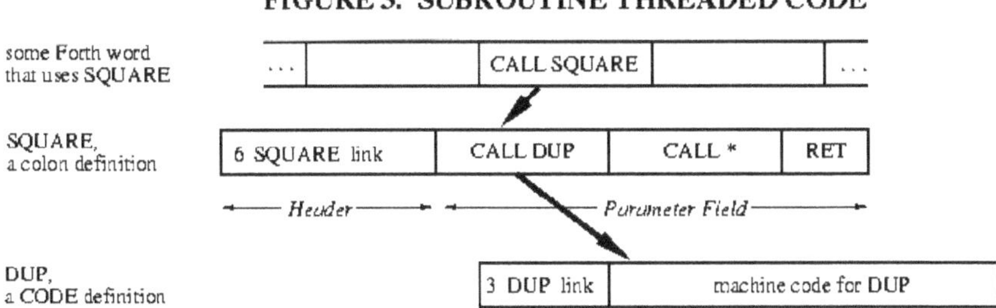

STC is an elegant representation; colon definitions and CODE words are now identical. "Defined words" (VARIABLEs, CONSTANTs, and the like) are handled the same as in DTC -- the Code Field begins with a jump or call to some machine code elsewhere.

The major disadvantage is that subroutine calls are usually larger than simple addresses. On the Z80, for example, the size of colon definitions increases by 50% -- and most of your application is colon definitions! Contrariwise, on a 32-bit 68000 there may be no size increase at all, when 4-byte addresses are replaced with 4-byte BSRs. (But if your code size exceeds 64K, some of those addresses must be replaced with 6-byte JSRs.)

Subroutine threading <u>may</u> be faster than direct threading. You save time by not having an interpreter, but you lose time because <u>every</u> reference to a Forth word involves a push and pop of a return address. In a DTC Forth, only high-level words cause activity on the return stack. On the 6809 or Zilog Super8, DTC is faster than STC.

There is another advantage to STC: it dispenses with the IP register. Some processors -- like the 8051 -- are desperately short of addressing registers. Eliminating the IP can really simplify and speed up the kernel!

<u>The only way to know for sure is to write sample code.</u> This is intimately involved with register selection, discussed in the next section.

1.9 STC with in-line expansion; optimization; direct compilation

On older and 8-bit CPUs, almost every Forth primitive involves several machine instructions. But on more powerful CPUs, many Forth primitives are written in a single instruction. For example, on the 32-bit 68000, DROP is simply

ADDQ #4,An   where An is Forth's PSP register

In a subroutine-threaded Forth, using DROP in a colon definition would result in the sequence

BSR ...		
BSR DROP	------->	DROP: ADDQ #4,An
BSR ...	<-------	RTS

ADDQ is a two-byte instruction. Why write a four-byte subroutine call to a two-byte instruction? No matter how many times DROP is used, there's no savings! The code is smaller and faster if the ADDQ is coded directly into the stream of BSRs. Some Forth compilers do this "in-line expansion" of CODE words [CUR93a].

The disadvantage of in-line expansion is that decompiling back to the original source code becomes very difficult. As long as subroutine calls are used, you still have pointers (the subroutine addresses) to the Forth words comprising the thread. With pointers to the words, you can obtain their names. But once a word is expanded into in-line code, all knowledge of where that code came from is lost.

The advantage of in-line expansion -- aside from speed and size -- is the potential for code optimization. For example, the Forth sequence

3 +

would be compiled in 68000 STC as

BSR	LIT
.DW	3
BSR	PLUS

but could be expanded in-line as a single machine instruction!

Optimizing Forth compilers is too broad a topic for this article. This is an active area of Forth language research; see, for instance, [SCO89] and [CUR93b]. The final culmination of optimized STC is a Forth which compiles to "pure" machine code, just like a C or Fortran compiler.

1.10 Token Threaded Code (TTC)

DTC and STC aim to improve the speed of Forth programs, at some cost in memory. Now let's move the other direction from ITC, toward something slower but smaller.

The purpose of a Forth thread is to specify a list of Forth words (subroutines) to be performed. Suppose a 16-bit Forth system only had a maximum of 256 different words. Then each word could be uniquely identified by an 8-bit number. Instead of a list of 16-bit addresses, you would have a list of 8-bit identifiers or "tokens," and the size of the colon definitions would be halved!
A token-threaded Forth keeps a table of addresses of all Forth words, as shown in Figure 4. The token value is then used to index into this table, to find the Forth word corresponding to a given token. This adds one level of indirection to the Forth interpreter, so it is slower than an "address-threaded" Forth.

FIGURE 4. TOKEN THREADED CODE

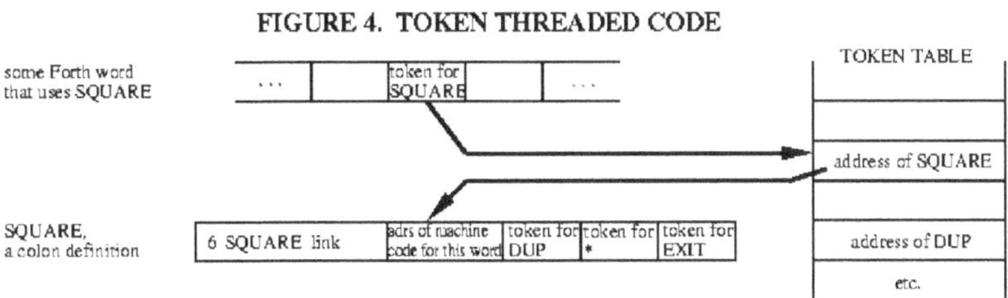

The principal advantage of token-threaded Forths is small size. TTC is most commonly seen in handheld computers and other severely size-constrained applications. Also, the table of "entry points" into all the Forth words can simplify linkage of separately-compiled modules.
The disadvantage of TTC is speed: TTC makes the slowest Forths. Also, the TTC compiler is slightly more complex. If you need more than 256 Forth words, it's necessary to have some open-ended encoding scheme to mix 8-bit and larger tokens. I can envision a 32-bit Forth using 16-bit tokens, but how many 32-bit systems are size-constrained?

1.11 Segment Threaded Code

Since there are so many 8086 derivatives in the world, segment threading deserves a brief mention. Instead of using "normal" byte addresses within a 64K segment, paragraph addresses are used. (A "paragraph" is 16 bytes in the 8086.) Then, the interpreter can load these addresses into segment registers, instead of into the usual address registers. This allows a 16- bit Forth model to efficiently access the full megabyte of 8086 memory.
The principal disadvantage of segment threading is the 16-byte "granularity" of the memory space. Every Forth word must be aligned to a 16-byte boundary. If Forth words have random lengths, an average of 8 bytes will be wasted per Forth word.

1.12 REGISTER ALLOCATION

Next to the threading technique, the usage of the CPU's registers is the most crucial design decision. It's probably the most difficult. The availability of CPU registers can determine what threading technique can be used, and even what the memory map will be!

1.13 The Classical Forth Registers

The classical Forth model has five "virtual registers." These are abstract entities which are used in the primitive operations of Forth. NEXT, ENTER, and EXIT were defined earlier in terms of these abstract registers.

Each of these is one cell wide -- i.e., in a 16-bit Forth, these are 16-bit registers. (There are exceptions to this rule, as you will see later.) These may not all be CPU registers. If your CPU doesn't have enough registers, some of these can be kept in memory. I'll describe them in the order of their importance; i.e., the bottom of this list are the best candidates to be stored in memory.

W is the Working register. It is used for many things, including memory reference, so it should be an address register; i.e., you must be able to fetch and store memory using the contents of W as the address. You also need to be able to do arithmetic on W. (In DTC Forths, you must also be able to jump indirect using W.) W is used by the interpreter in every Forth word. In a CPU having only one register, you would use it for W and keep everything else in memory (and the system would be incredibly slow).

IP is the Interpreter Pointer. This is used by every Forth word (through NEXT, ENTER, or EXIT). IP must be an address register. You also need to be able to increment IP. Subroutine threaded Forths don't need this register.

PSP is the Parameter Stack (or "data stack") Pointer, sometimes called simply SP. I prefer PSP because SP is frequently the name of a CPU register, and they shouldn't be confused. Most CODE words use this. PSP must be a stack pointer, or an address register which can be incremented and decremented. It's also a plus if you can do indexed addressing from PSP.

RSP is the Return Stack Pointer, sometimes called simply RP. This is used by colon definitions in ITC and DTC Forths, and by all words in STC Forths. RSP must be a stack pointer, or an address register which can be incremented and decremented.

If at all possible, put W, IP, PSP, and RSP in registers. The virtual registers that follow can be kept in memory, but there is usually a speed advantage to keeping them in CPU registers.

X is a working register, not considered one of the "classical" Forth registers, even though the classical ITC Forths need it for the second indirection. In ITC you must be able to jump indirect using X. X may also be used by a few CODE words to do arithmetic and such. This is particularly important on processors that cannot use memory as an operand. For example, ADD on a Z80 might be (in pseudo-code)

POP W POP X X+W -> W PUSH W

Sometimes another working register, Y, is also defined.
UP is the User Pointer, holding the base address of the task's user area. UP is usually added to an offset, and used by high-level Forth code, so it can be just stored somewhere. But if the CPU can do indexed addressing from the UP register, CODE words can more easily and quickly access user variables. If you have a surplus of address registers, use one for UP. Single-task Forths don't need UP.
X -- if needed -- is more important to keep in register than UP. UP is the easiest of the Forth virtual registers to move into memory.

1.14 Use of the Hardware Stack

Most CPUs have a stack pointer as part of their hardware, used by interrupts and subroutine calls. How does this map into the Forth registers? Should it be the PSP or the RSP?
The short answer is, it depends. It is said that the PSP is used more than the RSP in ITC and DTC Forths. If your CPU has few address registers, and PUSH and POP are faster than explicit reference, use the hardware stack as the Parameter Stack.
On the other hand, if your CPU is rich in addressing modes -- and allows indexed addressing -- there's a plus in having the PSP as a general-purpose address register. In this case, use the hardware stack as the Return Stack.
Sometimes you do neither! The TMS320C25's hardware stack is only eight cells deep -- all but useless for Forth. So its hardware stack is used only for interrupts, and both PSP and RSP are general-purpose address registers. (ANS Forth specifies a minimum of 32 cells of Parameter Stack and 24 cells of Return Stack; I prefer 64 cells of each.)
You will occasionally encounter the dogma that the hardware stack "must be" the Parameter Stack, or "must be" the Return Stack. Instead, code some sample Forth primitives, such as

SWAP OVER @ ! + 0=

and see which approach is smaller or faster. (DUP and DROP, by the way, are no test -- they're usually trivial.)
Occasionally you reach strange conclusions! Gary Bergstrom has pointed out that a 6809 DTC Forth can be made a few cycles faster by using the 6809 user stack pointer as the IP; NEXT becomes a POP. He uses an index register for one of Forth's stacks.

1.15 Top-Of-Stack in Register

Forth's performance can be improved considerably by keeping the top element of the Parameter Stack in a register! Many Forth words (such as 0=) then don't need to use the stack. Other words still do the same number of pushes and pops, only in a different place in the code. Only a few Forth words (DROP and 2DROP) become more complicated, since you can no longer simply adjust the stack pointer -- you have to update the TOS register as well.

There are a few rules when writing CODE words:

A word which removes items from the stack must pop the "new" TOS into its register.

A word which adds items to the stack must push the "old" TOS onto the stack (unless, of course, it's consumed by the word).

If you have at least six cell-size CPU registers, I recommend keeping the TOS in a register. I consider TOS more important than UP to have in register, but less important than W, IP, PSP, and RSP. (TOS in register performs many of the functions of the X register.) It's useful if this register can perform memory addressing. PDP-11s, Z8s, and 68000s are good candidates.

Nine of the 19 IBM PC Forths studied by Guy Kelly [KEL92] keep TOS in register.

I think this innovation has been resisted because of the false beliefs that a) it adds instructions, and b) the top stack element must be accessible as memory. It turns out that even such words as PICK, ROLL, and DEPTH are trivially modified for TOS-in-register.

What about buffering two stack elements in registers? When you keep the top of stack in a register, the total number of operations performed remains essentially the same. A push remains a push, regardless of whether it is before or after the operation you're performing. On the other hand, buffering two stack elements in registers adds a large number of instructions -- a push becomes a push followed by a move. Only dedicated Forth processors like the RTX2000 and fantastically clever optimizing compilers can benefit from buffering two stack elements in registers.

1.16 Some examples

Here are the register assignments made by Forths for a number of different CPUs. Try to deduce the design decisions of the authors from this list.

Figure 5. Register Assignments

	W	IP	PSP	RSP	UP	TOS	
8086[1]	BX	SI	SP	BP	memory	memory	[LAX84]
8086[2]	AX	SI	SP	BP	none	BX	[SER90]
68000	A5	A4	A3	A7=SP	A6	memory	[CUR86]

PDP-11	R2	R4	R5	R6=SP	R3	memory	[JAM80]
6809	X	Y	U	S	memory	memory	[TAL80]
6502	Zpage	Zpage	X	SP	Zpage	memory	[KUN81]
Z80	DE	BC	SP	IX	none	memory	[LOE81]
Z8	RR6	RR12	RR14	SP	RR10	RR8	[MPE92]
8051	R0,1	R2,3	R4,5	R6,7	fixed	memory	[PAY90]
[1] F83. [2] Pygmy Forth.							

"SP" refers to the hardware stack pointer. "Zpage" refers to values kept in the 6502's memory page zero, which are almost as useful as -- sometimes more useful than -- values kept in registers; e.g., they can be used for memory addressing. "Fixed" means that Payne's 8051 Forth has a single, immovable user area, and UP is a hard-coded constant.

1.17 Narrow Registers

Notice anything odd in the previous list? The 6502 Forth -- a 16-bit model -- uses 8-bit stack pointers!

It is possible to make PSP, RSP, and UP smaller than the cell size of the Forth. This is because the stacks and user area are both relatively small areas of memory. Each stack may be as small as 64 cells in length, and the user area rarely exceeds 128 cells. You simply need to ensure that either a) these data areas are confined to a small area of memory, so a short address can be used, or b) the high address bits are provided in some other way, e.g., a memory page select.

In the 6502, the hardware stack is confined to page one of RAM (addresses 01xxh) by the design of the CPU. The 8-bit stack pointer can be used for the Return Stack. The Parameter Stack is kept in page zero of RAM, which can be indirectly accessed by the 8-bit index register X. (Question for the advanced student: why use the 6502's X, and not Y? Hint: look at the addressing modes available.)

In the 8051, you can use the 8-bit registers R0 and R1 to address external RAM, provided that you explicitly output the high 8 bits of address to port 2. This allows a "page select" for two stacks.

UP is different from PSP and RSP: it simply provides a base address; it is never incremented or decremented. So it's practical to supply only the high bits of this virtual register. The low bits must then be provided by whatever indexed addressing technique is used. For example, on the 6809, you can use the DP register to hold the high 8 bits of UP, and then use Direct Page addressing to access any of the 256 locations in this page. This forces all user areas to begin on an address xx00h, which is no great hardship, and limits the user area to 128 cells in length.

On the 8086 you could conceivably use a segment register to specify the base address of the user area.

REFERENCES

[CUR93a] Curley, Charles, "Life in the FastForth Lane," awaiting publication in Forth Dimensions. Description of a 68000 subroutine-threaded Forth.

[CUR93b] Curley, Charles, "Optimizing in a BSR/JSR Threaded Forth," awaiting publication in Forth Dimensions. Single-pass code optimization for FastForth, in only five screens of code! Includes listing.

[KEL92] Kelly, Guy M., "Forth Systems Comparisons," Forth Dimensions XIII:6 (Mar/Apr 1992). Also published in the 1991 FORML Conference Proceedings. Both available from the Forth Interest Group, P.O. Box 2154, Oakland, CA 94621. Illustrates design tradeoffs of many 8086 Forths with code fragments and benchmarks -- highly recommended!

[KOG82] Kogge, Peter M., "An Architectural Trail to Threaded- Code Systems," IEEE Computer, vol. 15 no. 3 (Mar 1982). Remains the definitive description of various threading techniques.

[ROD91] Rodriguez, B.J., "B.Y.O. Assembler," Part 1, The Computer Journal #52 (Sep/Oct 1991). General principles of writing Forth assemblers.

[ROD92] Rodriguez, B.J., "B.Y.O. Assembler," Part 2, The Computer Journal #54 (Jan/Feb 1992). A 6809 assembler in Forth.

[SCO89] Scott, Andrew, "An Extensible Optimizer for Compiling Forth," 1989 FORML Conference Proceedings, **Forth Interest Group,** P.O. Box 2154, Oakland, CA 94621. Good description of a 68000 optimizer; no code provided.

Forth Implementations

[CUR86] Curley, Charles, real-Forth for the 68000, privately distributed (1986).

[JAM80] James, John S., fig-Forth for the PDP-11, Forth Interest Group (1980).

[KUN81] Kuntze, Robert E., MVP-Forth for the Apple II, Mountain View Press (1981).

[LAX84] Laxen, H. and Perry, M., F83 for the IBM PC, version 2.1.0 (1984). Distributed by the authors, available from the Forth Interest Group or GEnie.

[LOE81] Loeliger, R. G., Threaded Interpretive Languages, BYTE Publications (1981), ISBN 0-07-038360-X. May be the only book ever written on the subject of creating a Forth-like kernel (the example used is the Z80). Worth it if you can find a copy.

[MPE92] MicroProcessor Engineering Ltd., MPE Z8/Super8 PowerForth Target, MPE Ltd., 133 Hill Lane, Shirley, Southampton, S01 5AF, U.K. (June 1992). A commercial product.

[PAY90] Payne, William H., Embedded Controller FORTH for the 8051 Family, Academic Press (1990), ISBN 0-12-547570-5. This is a complete "kit" for a 8051 Forth,

including a metacompiler for the IBM PC. Hardcopy only; files can be downloaded from GEnie. Not for the novice!
[SER90] Sergeant, Frank, Pygmy Forth for the IBM PC, version 1.3 (1990). Distributed by the author, available from the Forth Interest Group. Version 1.4 is now available on GEnie, and worth the extra effort to obtain.
[TAL80] Talbot, R. J., fig-Forth for the 6809, Forth Interest Group (1980).

Author's note for web publication: the files formerly available on the GEnie online service are now available from the Forth Interest Group FTP server, ftp://ftp.forth.org/pub/Forth.
Continue with Part 2 | Back to publications page

MOVING FORTH by Brad Rodriguez

Part 2: Benchmarks and Case Studies of Forth Kernels

This article first appeared in **The Computer Journal** #60 (March/April 1993).

BENCHMARKS

By now it must seem that the answer to every design question is "code it and see." Obviously you don't want to write the entire Forth kernel several different ways just to evaluate different schemes. Fortunately, you can get quite a good "feel" with just a small subset of the Forth kernel.

Guy Kelly [KEL92] examines the following code samples for 19 different IBM PC Forths:

NEXT ...the "inner interpreter" that chains from one Forth word to another in the "thread". This is used at the end of every CODE definition, and is one of the most important factors in speed of Forth execution. You've already seen the pseudo-code for this in ITC and DTC; in STC it's just CALL/RETURN.

ENTER ...also called DOCOL or DOCOLON; the Code Field action that causes a high level "colon" definition to be executed. This, too, is crucial for speed; it is used at the start of every colon definition. Not needed in STC.

EXIT ...called ;S in fig-Forth; the code that ends the execution of a colon definition. This is essentially the high-level subroutine return, and appears at the end of every colon definition. This is just a machine code RETURN in STC.

NEXT, ENTER, and EXIT indicate the performance of the threading mechanism. These should be coded to evaluate ITC vs. DTC vs. STC. They also reflect the quality of your register assignments for IP, W, and RSP.

DOVAR ...a.k.a. "variable"; the machine code fragment that is the Code Field action for all Forth VARIABLEs.

DOCON ...a.k.a. "constant"; the machine code fragment that is the Code Field action for all Forth CONSTANTs.

DOCON and DOVAR, along with ENTER, show how efficiently you can obtain the Parameter Field address of a word being executed. This reflects your choice for the W register. In a DTC Forth, this also indicates whether to put a JUMP or CALL in the Code Field.

LIT ...a.k.a. "literal"; is a Forth word that fetches a cell value from the high-level thread. Several words use such in-line parameters, and this is a good indicator of their performance. It reflects your choice for the IP register.

@ ...the Forth memory-fetch operator, shows how quickly memory can be accessed from high-level Forth. This word usually benefits from TOS in stack.

! ...the Forth memory-store operator, is another indicator of memory access. This consumes two items from the stack, and illustrates efficiency of Parameter Stack access. It's a good indicator of the TOS-in-memory vs. TOS-in-register tradeoff.
+ ...the addition operator, is a representative example of all the Forth arithmetic and logical operators. Like the ! word, this benchmarks stack access, and it's a clear demonstration of any TOS-in-register benefit.
This is an excellent set of code samples. I have a few additional favorites:

DODOES ...is the Code Field action for words built with DOES>. This doesn't yield any new benchmark comparisons, although it does reflect the usefulness of W, IP, and RSP. I include it because it's the most convoluted code in the Forth kernel. If you can code the logic of DODOES, everything else is a snap. The intricacies of DODOES will be described in a subsequent article.

SWAP ...a simple stack operator, but still educational.

OVER ...a more complex stack operator. This gives a good idea of how easily you can access the Parameter Stack.

ROT ...a still more complex stack operator, and the one most likely to need an extra temporary register. If you can code ROT without needing an "X" register, you probably don't need an "X" register for anything.

0= ...one of the few unary arithmetic operators, and one of the most likely to benefit from TOS-in-register.

+! ...a most illustrative operator, combining stack access, arithmetic, memory fetch and store. This is one of my favorite benchmarks, although it is less frequently used than the other words in this list.
These are among the most-used words in the Forth kernel. It pays to optimize them. I'll show examples of all of these, including pseudo-code, for the 6809. For the other CPUs, I'll use selected examples to illustrate specific decisions.

CASE STUDY 1: THE 6809

In the world of 8-bit CPUs, the 6809 is the Forth programmer's dream machine. It supports two stacks! It also has two other address registers, and a wealth of orthogonal addressing modes second only to the PDP-11. ("Orthogonal" means they work the same way and have the same options for all address registers.) The two 8-bit accumulators can be treated as a single 16-bit accumulator, and there are many 16-bit operations.

The programmer's model of the 6809 is [MOT83]:

A - 8 bit accumulator
B - 8 bit accumulator

Most arithmetic operations use an accumulator as the destination. These can be concatenated and treated as a single 16-bit accumulator D (A high byte, B low).

X - 16 bit index register
Y - 16 bit index register
S - 16 bit stack pointer
U - 16 bit stack pointer

All addressing modes for X and Y can also be used with the S and U registers.

PC - 16 bit program counter
CC - 8 bit Condition Code register
DP - 8 bit Direct Page register

The 6800 family's Direct addressing mode uses an 8-bit address to reach any location in memory page zero. The 6809 allows any page to be Direct-addressed; this register provides the high 8 bits of address.

Those two stack pointers are crying out for Forth use. They are equivalent, except that S is used for subroutine calls and interrupts. Let's be consistent and use S for return addresses, leaving U for the Parameter Stack.

W and IP both need to be address registers, so these are the logical use for X and Y. X and Y are equivalent, so let's arbitrarily assign X=W, and Y=IP.

Now a threading model can be chosen. I'll scratch STC and TTC, to make this a "conventional" Forth. The limiting factor in performance is then the NEXT routine. Let's look at this in both ITC and DTC:

ITC-NEXT:	LDX ,Y++	(8) (IP)->W, increment IP
	JMP [,X]	(6) (W)->temp, jump to adrs in temp

DTC-NEXT:	JMP [,Y++]	(9) (IP)->temp, increment IP, jump to adrs in temp ("temp" is internal to the 6809)

NEXT is one instruction in a DTC 6809! This means you can code it in-line in two bytes, making it both smaller and faster than JMP NEXT. For comparison, look at the "NEXT" logic for subrou~ tine threading:

	RTS	(5) ...at the end of one CODE word
	JSR nextword	(8) ...in the "thread"
	...	...start of the next CODE word

STC takes 13 clocks to thread to the next word, compared with 9 clocks for DTC. This is because subroutine threading has to pop and push a return address, while simple DTC or ITC threading between CODE words does not.
Given the choice of DTC, you have to decide: does a high-level word have a Jump or Call in its Code Field? The driving consid~ eration is <u>how quickly can you obtain the address of the parame~ ter field which follows?</u> Let's look at the code to ENTER a colon definition, using symbolic Forth register names, to see this illustrated:
using a JSR (Call):

	JSR ENTER	(8)
	...	
ENTER:	PULS W	(7) get address following JSR into W reg
	PSHS IP	(7) save the old IP on the Return Stack
	TFR W,IP	(6) Parameter Field address -> IP
	NEXT	(9) assembler macro for JMP [,Y++]
		37 cycles total

using a JMP:

	JMP ENTER	(4)
	...	
ENTER:	PSHS IP	(7) save the old IP on the Return Stack
	LDX -2,IP	(6) re-fetch the Code Field address
	LEAY 3,X	(5) add 3 and put into IP (Y) register

	NEXT	(9)
		31 cycles total
		(CPU cycle counts are in parentheses.)

The DTC 6809 NEXT doesn't use the W register, because the 6809 addressing modes allow an extra level of indirection automatically. The JMP version of ENTER has to re-fetch the Code Field address -- NEXT didn't leave it in any register -- and then add 3 to get the Parameter Field address. The JSR version can get the Parameter Field address directly by popping the return stack. Even so, the JMP version is faster. (Exercise for the student: try coding the JSR ENTER with S=PSP and U=RSP.)
Either way, the code for EXIT is the same:

EXIT:	PULS IP	pop "saved" IP from return stack
	NEXT	continue Forth interpretation

Some registers remain to allocate. You could keep the User Pointer in memory, and this Forth would still be pretty fast. But the DP register would go to waste, and there's not much else it can do. Let's use the "trick" described above, and hold the high byte of UP in the DP register. (The low byte of UP is implied to be zero).
One 16-bit register is left: D. Most arithmetic operations need this register. Should it be left free as a scratch register, or used as the Top-Of-Stack? 6809 instructions use memory as one operand, so a second working register may be unnecessary. And if a scratch register is needed, it's easy to push and pop D. Let's write the benchmark primitives both ways, and see which is faster.
NEXT, ENTER, and EXIT don't use the stack, and thus have identical code either way. DOVAR, DOCON, LIT, and OVER require the same number of CPU cycles either way. These illustrate the earlier comment that putting TOS in register often just changes where the push or pop takes place:

	TOS in D	TOS in memory	pseudo-code
DOVAR:	PSHU TOS	LDD -2,IP	address of CF -> D
	LDD -2,IP	ADDD #3	address of PF -> D
	ADDD #3	PSHU D	push D onto stack
	NEXT	NEXT	

	TOS in D	TOS in memory	pseudo-code
DOCON:	PSHU TOS	LDX -2,IP	address of CF -> W
	LDX -2,IP	LDD 3,X	contents of PF -> D
	LDD 3,X	PSHU D	push D onto stack
	NEXT	NEXT	

	TOS in D	TOS in memory	pseudo-code
LIT:	PSHU TOS	LDD ,IP++	9IP) -> D, increment IP
	LDD ,IP++	PSHU D	push D onto stack
	NEXT	NEXT	

	TOS in D	TOS in memory	pseudo-code
OVER:	PSHU D	LDD 2,PSP	2nd on stack -> D
	LDD 2,PSP	PSHU D	push D onto stack
	NEXT	NEXT	

SWAP, ROT, 0=, @, and especially + are all faster with TOS in register:

	TOS in D	TOS in memory	pseudo-code
SWAP:	LDX ,PSP (5)	LDD ,PSP (5)	TOS -> D
	STD ,PSP (5)	LDX 2,PSP (6)	2nd on stack -> X
	TFR X,D (6)	STD 2,PSP (6)	D -> 2nd on stack
	NEXT	STX ,PSP (5)	X -> TOS
		NEXT	

	TOS in D	TOS in memory	pseudo-code
ROT:	LDX ,PSP (5)	LDX ,PSP (5)	TOS -> X
	STD ,PSP (5)	LDD 2,PSP (6)	2nd on stack -> D
	LDD 2,PSP (6)	STX 2,PSP (6)	X -> 2nd on stack
	STX 2,PSP (6)	LDX 4,PSP (6)	3rd on stack -> X
	NEXT	STD 4,PSP (6)	D -> 3rd on stack
		STX ,PSP (5)	X -> TOS
		NEXT	

	TOS in D	TOS in memory	pseudo-code
0=:	CMPD #0	LDD ,PSP	TOS -> D
	BEQ TRUE	CMPD #0	does D equal zero?
		BEQ TRUE	
FALSE:	LDD #0	LDD #0	no...put 0 in TOS
	NEXT	STD ,PSP	
		NEXT	
TRUE:	LDD #-1	LDD #-1	yes...put -1 in TOS
	NEXT	STD ,PSP	

		NEXT	

	TOS in D	TOS in memory	pseudo-code
@:	TFR TOS,W (6)	LDD [,PSP] (8)	fetch D using TOS adrs
	LDD ,W (5)	STD ,PSP (5)	D -> TOS
	NEXT	NEXT	

	TOS in D	TOS in memory	pseudo-code
+:	ADDD ,U++	PULU D	pop TOS into D
	NEXT	ADDD ,PSP	add new TOS into D
		STD ,PSP	store D into TOS
		NEXT	

! and +! are <u>slower</u> with TOS in register:

	TOS in D	TOS in memory	pseudo-code
!:	TFR TOS,W (6)	PULU W (7)	pop adrs into W
	PULU D (7)	PULU D (7)	pop data into D
	STD ,W (5)	STD ,W (5)	store data to adrs
	PULU TOS (7)	NEXT	
	NEXT		

	TOS in D	TOS in memory	pseudo-code
+!:	TFR TOS,W (6)	PULU W (7)	pop adrs into W
	PULU TOS (7)	PULU D (7)	pop data into D
	ADDD ,W (6)	ADDD ,W (6)	add memory into D
	STD ,W (5)	STD ,W (5)	store D to memory
	PULU TOS (7)	NEXT	
	NEXT		

The reason these words are slower is that most Forth memory- reference words expect the address on the top of stack, so an extra TFR instruction is needed. This is why it's a help for the TOS register to be an address register. Unfortunately, all the 6809 address registers are spoken for...and it's much more important for W, IP, PSP, and RSP to be in address registers than TOS. The TOS-in-register penalty for ! and +! should be outweighed by the gains in the many arithmetic and stack operations.

CASE STUDY 2: THE 8051

If the 6809 is the Forthwright's dream machine, the 8051 is the nightmare. It has only one general-purpose address register, and one addressing mode, which always uses the one 8-bit accumulator.

All of the arithmetic operations, and many of the logical, must use the accumulator. The only 16-bit operation is INC DPTR. The hardware stack must use the 128-byte on-chip register file. [SIG92] Such a CPU could give ulcers.

Some 8051 Forths have been written that implement a full 16-bit model, e.g. [PAY90], but they are too slow for my taste. Let's make some tradeoffs and make a faster 8051 Forth.

Our foremost reality is the availability of only one address register. So let's use the 8051's Program Counter as IP -- i.e., let's make a subroutine-threaded Forth. If the compiler uses 2- byte ACALLs instead of 3-byte LCALLs whenever possible, most of the STC code will be as small as ITC or DTC code.

Subroutine threading implies that the Return Stack Pointer is the hardware stack pointer. There are 64 cells of space in the on- chip register file, not enough room for multiple task stacks. At this point you can

a) restrict this Forth to single-task;

b) code all of the Forth definitions so that upon entry they move their return address to a software stack in external RAM; or

c) do task switches by swapping the entire Return Stack to and from external RAM.
Option (b) is slow! Moving 128 bytes on every task switch is faster than moving 2 bytes on every Forth word. For now I choose option (a), leaving the door open for (c) at some future date.

The one-and-only "real" address register, DPTR, will have to do multiple duty. It becomes W, the multi-purpose working register.

In truth, there are two other registers that can address external memory: R0 and R1. They provide only an 8-bit address; the high 8 bits are explicitly output on port 2. But this is a tolerable restriction for stacks, since they can be limited to a 256-byte space. So let's use R0 as the PSP.

This same 256-byte space can be used for user data. This makes P2 (port 2) the high byte of the User Pointer, and, like the 6809, the low byte will be implied to be zero.

What is the programmer's model of the 8051 so far?

reg adrs	8051 name	Forth usage
0	R0	low byte of PSP
1	R1	
2	R2	
3	R3	
4	R4	
5	R5	
6	R6	
7	R7	
8 -	7Fh	120 bytes of return stack
81h	SP	low byte of RSP (high byte=00)
82 -	83h	DPTR W register
A0h	P2	high byte of UP and PSP
E0h	A	
F0h	B	

Note that this uses only register bank 0. The additional three register banks from 08h to 1Fh, and the bit-addressable region from 20h to 2Fh, are of no use to Forth. Using bank 0 leaves the largest contiguous space for the return stack. Later the return stack can be shrunk, if desired.

The NEXT, ENTER, and EXIT routines aren't needed in a subroutine threaded Forth.

What about the top of stack? There are plenty of registers, and memory operations on the 8051 are expensive. Let's put TOS in R3:R2 (with R3 as the high byte, in Intel fashion). Note that B:A can't be used -- the A register is the funnel through which all memory references must move!

Harvard architectures

The 8051 uses a "Harvard" architecture: program and data are kept in separate memories. (The Z8 and TMS320 are two other examples.) The 8051 is a degenerate case: there is physically no means to write to the program memory! This means that a Forthwright can do one of two things:

a) cross-compile everything, including the application, and give up all hope of putting an interactive Forth compiler on the 8051; or

b) cause some or all of the program memory to also appear in the data space. The easiest way is to make the two spaces completely overlap, by logically ORing the active-low PSEN* and RD* strobes with an external AND gate.

The Z8 and TMS320C25 are more civilized: they allow write access to program memory. The implications for the design of the Forth kernel will be discussed in subsequent articles.

CASE STUDY 3: THE Z80

The Z80 is instructive because it is an extreme example of a non- orthogonal CPU. It has four different kinds of address registers! Some operations use A as destination, some any 8-bit register, some HL, some any 16-bit register, and so on. Many operations (such as EX DE,HL) are only defined for one combination of registers.

In a CPU such as the Z80 (or 8086!), the assignment of Forth functions must be carefully matched to the capabilities of the CPU registers. Many more tradeoffs need to be evaluated, and often the only way is to write sample code for a number of different assignments. Rather than burden this article down endless permutations of Forth code, I'll present one register assignment based on many Z80 code experiments. It turns out that these choices can be rationalized in terms of the general principles outlined earlier.

I want a "conventional" Forth, although I will use direct threading. All of the "classical" virtual registers will be needed.

Ignoring the alternate register set, the Z80 has six address registers, with the following capabilities:

BC,DE -	**LD A indirect, INC, DEC also exchange DE/HL**
HL -	**LD r indirect, ALU indirect, INC, DEC, ADD, ADC, SBC, exchange w/TOS, JP indirect**
IX,IY -	**LD r indexed, ALU indexed, INC, DEC, ADD, ADC, SBC, exchange w/TOS, JP indirect (all slow)**
SP -	**PUSH/POP 16-bit, ADD/ADC/SUB to HL/IX/IY**

BC, DE, and HL can also be manipulated in 8-bit pieces.

The 8-bit register A must be left as a scratch register, since it's the destination for so many ALU and memory reference operations.

HL is undoubtedly the most versatile register, and at one time or another it is tempting to use it for each of the Forth virtual registers. However, because of its versatility -- and because it is the only register which can be fetched byte-wise and used in an indirect jump -- HL should be used for W, Forth's all-purpose working register.

IX and IY might be considered for the Forth stack pointers, because of their indexed addressing mode, which can be used in ALU operations. But there are two problems with this: it leaves SP without a job; and, IX/IY are too slow! Most of the operations on either stack involve pushing or popping 16-bit quantities. This is one instruction using SP, but it requires four using IX or IY. One of the Forth stacks should use SP. And this should be the Parameter Stack, since it is used more heavily than the Return Stack.

What about Forth's IP? Mostly, IP fetches from memory and autoincrements, so there's no programming advantage to using IX/IY over BC/DE. But speed is of the essence with IP, and BC/DE are faster. Let's put IP in DE: it has the advantage of being able to swap with HL, which adds versatility.

A second Z80 register pair (other than W) will be needed for 16- bit arithmetic. Only BC is left, and it can be used for addressing or for ALU operations with A. But should BC be a second working register "X", or the top-of-stack? Only code will tell; for now, let's optimistically assume that BC=TOS.

This leaves the RSP and UP functions, and the IX and IY registers unused. IX and IY are equivalent, so let's assign IX=RSP, and IY=UP.

Thus the Z80 Forth register assignments are:

BC = TOS	IX = RSP
DE = IP	IY = UP
HL = W	SP = PSP

Now look at NEXT for the DTC Forth:

DTC-NEXT:	LD A,(DE) (7)	(IP)->W, increment IP
	LD L,A (4)	
	INC DE (6)	
	LD A,(DE) (7)	
	LD H,A (4)	
	INC DE (6)	
	JP (HL) (4)	jump to address in W

alternate version (same number of clock cycles)

DTC-NEXT:	EX DE,HL (4)	(IP)->W, increment IP
NEXT-HL:	LD E,(HL) (7)	
	INC HL (6)	
	LD D,(HL) (7)	
	INC HL (6)	
	EX DE,HL (4)	
	JP (HL) (4)	jump to address in W

Note that cells are stored low-byte first in memory. Also, although it might seem advantageous to keep IP in HL, it really isn't. This is because the Z80 can't JP (DE). The NEXT-HL entry point will be used shortly.

Just for comparison, let's look at an ITC NEXT. The pseudo-code given previously requires another temporary register "X", whose contents can be used for an indirect jump. Let DE=X, and BC=IP. TOS will have to be kept in memory.

ITC-NEXT:	LD A,(BC) (7)	(IP)->W, increment IP
	LD L,A (4)	
	INC BC (6)	
	LD A,(BC) (7)	
	LD H,A (4)	
	INC BC (6)	
	LD E,(HL) (7)	(W)->X
	INC HL (6)	
	LD D,(HL) (7)	
	EX DE,HL (4)	jump to address in X
	JP (HL) (4)	

This leaves "W" incremented by one, and in the DE register. As long as this is done consistently, there's no problem -- code needing the contents of W knows where to find it, and how much to adjust it.

The ITC NEXT is 11 instructions, as compared to 7 for DTC. And ITC on the Z80 loses the ability to keep TOS in a register. My choice is DTC.

If coded in-line, DTC NEXT would require seven bytes in every CODE word. A jump to a common NEXT routine would only use three bytes, but would add 10 clock cycles. This is another of the tradeoff decisions in designing a Forth kernel. This example is a close call; let's opt for speed with an in-line NEXT. But sometimes NEXT is so huge, or memory is so tight, that the prudent decision is to use a JMP NEXT.

Now let's look at the code for ENTER. Using a CALL, the hardware stack is popped to get the Parameter Field address:

	CALL ENTER (17)	
	...	
ENTER:	DEC IX	(10) push the old IP on the return stack
	LD (IX+0),D (19)	
	DEC IX (10)	

	LD (IX+0),E (19)	
	POP DE (10)	Parameter Field address -> IP
	NEXT (38)	assembler macro for 7 instructions

Actually it's faster to POP HL, and then use the last six instructions of NEXT (omitting the EX DE,HL):

	CALL ENTER (17)	
	...	
ENTER:	DEC IX (10)	push the old IP on the return stack
	LD (IX+0),D (19)	
	DEC IX (10)	
	LD (IX+0),E (19)	
	POP HL (10)	Parameter Field address -> HL
	NEXT-HL (34)	see DTC NEXT code, above
		119 cycles total

When a JP is used, the W register (HL) is left pointing to the Code Field. The Parameter Field is 3 bytes after:

	CALL ENTER (17)	
	...	
ENTER:	DEC IX (10)	push the old IP on the return stack
	LD (IX+0),D (19)	
	DEC IX (10)	
	LD (IX+0),E (19)	
	INC HL (6)	Parameter Field address -> IP
	INC HL (6)	
	INC HL (6)	
	NEXT-HL (34)	
		120 cycles total

Again, because of the alternate entry point for NEXT, the new value for IP doesn't actually have to be put into the DE register pair.
The CALL version is one cycle faster. On an embedded Z80, a one- byte RST instruction could be used to gain speed and save space. This option is not available on many Z80-based personal computers.

CASE STUDY 4: THE 8086

The 8086 is another instructive CPU. Rather than go through the design process, let's look at one of the newer shareware Forths for the IBM PC: Pygmy Forth [SER90]. Pygmy is a direct-threaded Forth with the top-of-stack kept in register. The 8086 register assignments are:

AX = W	**DI = scratch**
BX = TOS	**SI = IP**
CX = scratch	**BP = RSP**
DX = scratch	**SP = PSP**

Most 8086 Forths use the SI register for IP, so that NEXT can be written with the LODSW instruction. In Pygmy the DTC NEXT is:

NEXT:	**LODSW**
	JMP AX

This is short enough to include in-line in every CODE word.
High-level and "defined" Forth words use a JMP (relative) to their machine code. The ENTER routine (called 'docol' in Pygmy) must therefore get the Parameter Field address from W:

ENTER:	**XCHG SP,BP**	
	PUSH SI	
	XCHG SP,BP	
	ADD AX,3	**Parameter Field address -> IP**
	MOV SI,AX	
	NEXT	

Note the use of XCHG to swap the two stack pointers. This allows the use of PUSH and POP instructions for both stacks, which is faster than using indirect access on BP.

EXIT:	**XCHG SP,BP**
	POP SI
	XCHG SP,BP
	NEXT

Segment model

Pygmy Forth is a single-segment Forth; all code and data are contained within a single 64 Kbyte segment. (This is the "tiny model" in Turbo C lingo.) All of the Forth standards issued to date assume that everything is contained in a single memory space, accessible with the same fetch and store operators.
Nevertheless, IBM PC Forths are beginning to appear that use multiple segments for up to five different kinds of data [KEL92,SEY89]. These are:

CODE	. machine code
LIST	. high-level Forth threads (a.k.a. THREADS)
HEAD	. headers of all Forth words
STACK	. parameter and return stacks
DATA	.variables and user-defined data

This allows PC Forths to break the 64K limit, without going to the expense of implementing a 32-bit Forth on a 16-bit CPU. Implementation of a multi-segment model, and the ramifications for the Forth kernel, are beyond the scope of this article.

STILL TO COME...

Subsequent articles will look at:
- design tradeoffs in the Forth header and dictionary search
- the logic of CONSTANTs, VARIABLEs, and other data structures
- the defining word mechanisms, CREATE...;CODE and CREATE...DOES>
- the assembler vs. metacompiler question
- the assembler and high-level code that comprises a Forth kernel
- multitasking modifications to the kernel

REFERENCES

[KEL92] Kelly, Guy M., "Forth Systems Comparisons," Forth Dimensions XIII:6 (Mar/Apr 1992). Also published in the 1991 FORML Conference Proceedings. Both available from the Forth Interest Group, P.O. Box 2154, Oakland, CA 94621. Illustrates design tradeoffs of many 8086 Forths with code fragments and benchmarks -- highly recommended!

[MOT83] Motorola Inc., 8-Bit Microprocessor and Peripheral Data, Motorola data book (1983).

[SIG92] Signetics Inc., 80C51-Based 8-Bit Microcontrollers, Signetics data book (1992).

Forth Implementations

[PAY90] Payne, William H., Embedded Controller FORTH for the 8051 Family, Academic Press (1990), ISBN 0-12-547570-5. This is a complete "kit" for a 8051 Forth, including a metacompiler for the IBM PC. Hardcopy only; files can be downloaded from GEnie. Not for the novice!

[SER90] Sergeant, Frank, Pygmy Forth for the IBM PC, version 1.3 (1990). Distributed by the author, available from the Forth Interest Group. Version 1.4 is now available on GEnie, and worth the extra effort to obtain.

[SEY89] Seywerd, H., Elehew, W. R., and Caven, P., LOVE-83Forth for the IBM PC, version 1.20 (1989). A shareware Forth using a five-segment model. Contact Seywerd Associates, 265 Scarboro Cres., Scarborough, Ontario M1M 2J7 Canada.

Author's note for web publication: the files formerly available on the GEnie online service are now available from the Forth Interest Group FTP server, ftp://ftp.forth.org/pub/Forth.

Continue with Part 3 | Back to publications page

MOVING FORTH by Brad Rodriguez

Part 3: Demystifying DOES>

This article first appeared in **The Computer Journal** #62 (July/August 1993).

OOPS!

There's a colossal mistake in one of my 6809 design decisions in the previous installment. It became evident when I started to code the Forth word EXECUTE. EXECUTE causes the execution of a single Forth word, whose address is given on the Parameter Stack. (To be precise: the compilation address, a.k.a. Code Field Address, is given on the stack.) This can be any kind of Forth word: CODE definition, colon definition, CONSTANT, VARIABLE, or defined word. This differs from the usual Forth interpretation process in that the address of the word-to-execute is given on the stack, and not taken from the "thread" (as pointed to by IP).

In our direct-threaded 6809 code this can be easily coded:

EXECUTE:	TFR TOS,W	put address of word in W
	PULU TOS	pop new TOS
	JMP ,W	jump to address given in W

Note: this is JMP ,W and not JMP [,W], since we already have the code address of the word. We're not fetching from the high-level thread. (If TOS wasn't in register, EXECUTE could be done with simply JMP [,PSP++].) Now suppose that this EXECUTEd word is a colon definition. W will be pointing to its Code Field, which contains JMP ENTER. This does the following (described in the previous article):

	JMP ENTER	
	...	
ENTER:	PSHS IP	
	LDX -2,IP	re-fetch the Code Field address
	LEAY 3,X	
	NEXT	

This is the mistake! We are <u>not</u> executing this word from within a thread, so IP was <u>not</u> pointing to a copy of its Code Field address! (Remember, the address of the word-to-EXECUTE came from the <u>stack</u>.) This form of ENTER will not work with EXECUTE, because there is no way to find the address of the word being executed!

This suggests a new general rule for DTC Forths: if NEXT does NOT leave the address of the word-being-executed in a register, you MUST use a Call in the code field.
So, the 6809 Forth is back to using a JSR in the Code Field. But to avoid the speed penalty for ENTER -- one of the most-used code fragments in Forth -- I'll complete the "exercise for the student" from the last article. Note what happens if you swap the registers assigned to RSP and PSP:

	with RSP=S,	with RSP=U,	
	and PSP=U	and PSP=S	
	(previous)	(new)	
	JSR ENTER	JSR ENTER	
	...	...	
ENTER:	PULS W	PSHU IP	push old IP onto R stack
	PSHS IP	PULS IP	pop new IP from JSR stack
	TFR W,IP	NEXT	
	NEXT		

The new version executes in 31 cycles, the same as the JMP version I had wanted to use. The improvement is because the JSR version of ENTER must use both Forth's Return Stack, and the 6809 subroutine-return stack ("JSR stack"). Using two different stack pointers means we don't have to "swap" the top-of-stack with IP, eliminating the need for a temporary register.
This illustrates the usual development process for a new Forth kernel: make some design decisions, write some sample code, discover a bug or a better way to do things, throw out some code, change some design decisions, rewrite some sample code, loop until satisfied. (This is the programming equivalent of a "rip up" PC board autorouter.)
This teaches an important lesson: make EXECUTE one of your benchmark words!

OOPS, AGAIN

Carey Bloodworth of Van Buren, AR has pointed out a minor but embarassing mistake in my 6809 code in the previous installment. For the "TOS-in-memory" version of 0=, I showed the code fragment

	LDD ,PSP	
	CMPD #0	

to test for top-of-stack equalling zero. In this case, the CMPD instruction is completly superfluous, since the LDD instruction will set the Zero flag if D is zero! (The TOS-in-

D version still requires the CMPD instruction, but remains faster than TOS-in-memory.)
Now, on to our main topic:

WHAT'S A CODE FIELD?

The DOES> concept seems to be one of the most misunderstood and mystifying aspects of Forth. Yet DOES> is also one of Forth's most powerful features -- in many ways, it anticipated object- oriented programming. The action and power of DOES> hinges upon a brilliant innovation of Forth: the Code Field.
Recall from Part 1 that the "body" of a Forth definition consists of two parts: the Code Field, and the Parameter Field. You can think of these two fields in several ways:
* The Code Field is the "action" taken by this Forth word, and the Parameter Field is the data on which it acts.
* The Code Field is a subroutine call, and the Parameter Field is parameters that are included "in-line" after the call. (The assembly language programmer's view.)
* The Code Field is the single "method" for this "class" of words, and the Parameter Field contains the "instance variables" for this particular word. (The object-oriented programmer's view.)
Common features appear in all these views:
* The Code Field routine is always called with at least one argument, namely, the address of the Parameter Field for the Forth word being executed. The Parameter Field may contain any number of parameters.
* There are relatively few distinct actions, i.e., relatively few distinct routines referenced by the Code Field. Each of these routines is widely shared (except for CODE words, as we will see later). Recall, for example, the ENTER routine from Part 2: this common routine is used by all Forth colon definitions.
* The interpretation of the Parameter Field is implicitly determined by the contents of the Code Field. I.e., each Code Field routine expects the Parameter Field to contain a certain kind of data.
A typical Forth kernel will have several Code Field routines predefined.

Code Field routine	**Parameter Field contents**
ENTER	**a high-level "thread" (series of addresses)**
DOCON	**a constant value**
DOVAR	**a storage location for data**
DOVOC	**vocabulary info (varies by implementation)**

What makes this feature powerful is that a Forth program is not limited to this set of Code Field routines (or whatever set is provided in your kernel). The programmer can define new Code Field routines, and new Parameter Fields to match. In object-oriented lingo, new "classes" and "methods" can be created (although each class has only one method). And -- like Forth words themselves -- the Code Field actions can be defined in either assembly language or high-level Forth!

To understand the mechanism of the Code Field, and how parameters are passed, we will first look at the case of assembly-language (machine code) actions. We'll start with Indirect Threading (ITC), since it is the easiest to understand, and then see how the logic is modified in Direct-Threaded (DTC) and Subroutine- Threaded (STC) Forths. Then, we'll look at how the Code Field action can be written in high-level Forth.

Forthwrights are somewhat inconsistent in their terminology, so I'll define my terms, using the ITC Forth word illustrated in Figure 1. The Header contains the dictionary information, and isn't involved in the execution of the Forth word. The Body is the "working" part of the word, and consists of the fixed-length Code Field, and the variable-length Parameter Field.

For any given word, the locations of these two fields in memory are the Code Field Address (CFA) and the Parameter Field Address (PFA), respectively. The Code Field Address of a word is the address in memory where its Code Field is located. This is not to be confused with the contents of the Code Field, which, in ITC Forths, is another different address. To be specific, the contents of the Code Field is the address of a fragment of machine code somewhere else in memory. I will refer to this as the Code Address. Later, when in discussing DTC and STC Forths, I will also refer to the "Code Field contents," which will include more than just the Code Address.

FIGURE 1. AN ITC FORTH WORD

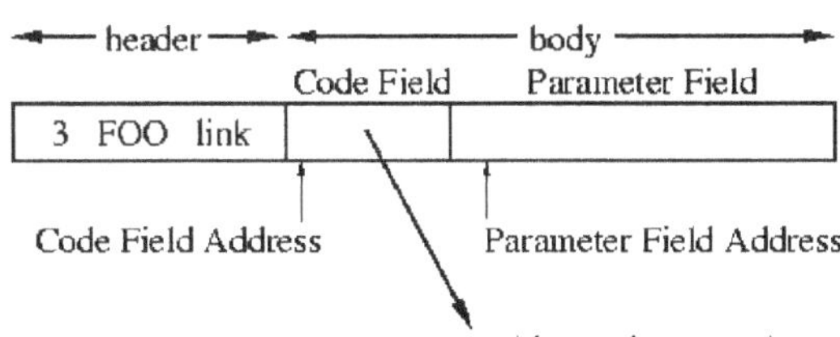

MACHINE-CODE ACTIONS

Forth CONSTANTs are probably the simplest example of a machine- code action. Let's consider some good Francophone constants

1 CONSTANT UN
2 CONSTANT DEUX
3 CONSTANT TROIS

Executing the word UN will push the value 1 onto the Forth Parameter Stack. Executing DEUX will push a 2 onto the stack, and so on. (Don't confuse Parameter Stack with Parameter Field; they are entirely separate.)

In the Forth kernel there is a single word called CONSTANT. This is not a constant-type word itself; it is a high-level Forth definition. CONSTANT is a "defining word": it creates new words in the Forth dictionary. Here we create the new "constant-type" words UN, DEUX, and TROIS. (You may think of these as "instances" of the "class" CONSTANT.) These three words will have their Code Fields pointing to a machine code fragment that does the action of CONSTANT.

What must this code fragment do? Figure 2 shows the memory representation of the three constants. All three words point to a common action routine. The difference in the words is entirely contained in their Parameter Fields, which, in this case, simply hold the constant values ("instance variables" in object lingo). So, the action of these three words should be fetch the contents of the Parameter Field, and push this onto the stack. The code understands implicitly that the parameter field contains a single-cell value.

FIGURE 2. THREE CONSTANTS

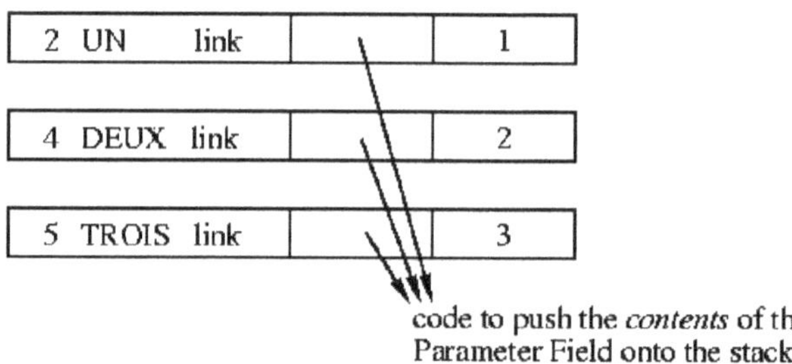

To write a machine-code fragment to do this, we need to know how to find the Parameter Field Address, after the Forth interepreter jumps to the machine code. That is, how is the PFA passed to the machine-code routine? This, in turn, depends on how the Forth interpreter NEXT has been coded, which varies from implementation to implementation. To write machine-code actions, we must understand NEXT.

The ITC NEXT was described in pseudo-code in Part 1. Here's one implementation for the 6809, using Y=IP and X=W:

NEXT:	LDX ,Y++	; (IP) -> W, and IP+2 -> IP
	JMP [,X]	; (W) -> temp, JMP (temp)

Suppose that we're in a high-level thread

... SWAP DEUX + ...

with the Interpreter Pointer (IP) pointing to the DEUX "instruction," when NEXT is executed. (This would be at the very end of SWAP.) Figure 3 illustrates what happens. IP (register Y) is pointing within the high-level thread, at a memory cell that contains the address of the Forth word DEUX. To be precise, this cell contains the Code Field Address of DEUX. So, when we fetch a cell using Y, and autoincrement Y, we fetch the Code Field Address of DEUX. This goes into W (register X), so W is now pointing to the Code Field.

The contents of this field is the address of some machine code. We can fetch the contents of this cell and jump to the machine code with a single 6809 instruction. This leaves register X unchanged, so W is still pointing to the CFA of DEUX. This is how the Parameter Field Address is obtained, since, in this case, it is simply two bytes past the Code Field.

FIGURE 3. ITC BEFORE AND AFTER "NEXT"

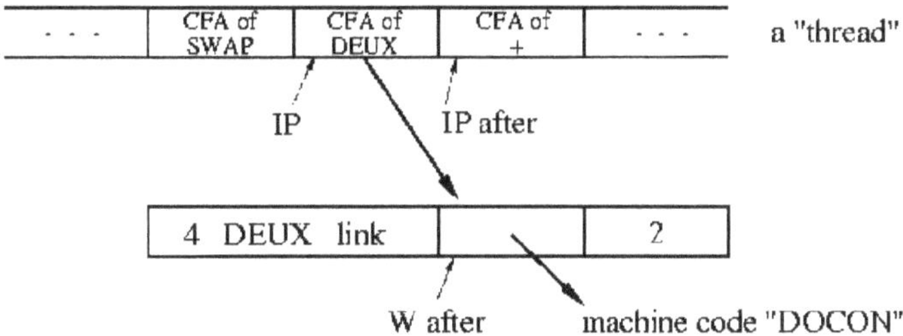

So, the machine code fragment has only to add 2 to W, fetch the cell value at that address, and push that on the stack. This fragment is frequently called DOCON:

DOCON:	LDD 2,X	; fetch the cell at W+2
	PSHU D	; push that on the Parameter Stack
	NEXT	; (macro) do the next high-level word

(For this example, TOS is kept in memory.) Note that the previous NEXT incremented IP by 2, so it is already pointing to the next cell in the thread ("CFA of +") when DOCON does NEXT.

In general, ITC Forths leave the Parameter Field Address or some "nearby" address in the W register. In this case, W contained the CFA, which in this Forth implementation is always PFA-2. Since every class of Forth word except CODE words needs to use the Parameter Field Address, many implementations of NEXT will increment W to leave it pointing to the PFA. We can do this on the 6809 with one small change:

NEXT:	LDX ,Y++	; (IP) -> W, and IP+2 -> IP
	JMP [,X++]	; (W) -> temp, JMP (temp), W+2 -> W

This adds three clock cycles to NEXT, and leaves the Parameter Field Address in W. What does it do to the Code Field routines?

	W=CFA	W=PFA
DOCON:	LDD 2,X (6)	LDD ,X (5)
	PSHU D	PSHU D
	NEXT	NEXT

	W=CFA	W=PFA	
DOVAR:	LEAX 2,X (5)		; no operation
	PSHU X	PSHU X	
	NEXT	NEXT	

	W=CFA	W=PFA	
ENTER:	PSHS Y	PSHS Y	
	LEAY 2,X (5)	LEAY ,X (4)	faster than TFR X,Y)
	NEXT	NEXT	

In exchange for a three-cycle penalty in NEXT, the DOCON code is reduced by one clock cycle, DOVAR by five cycles, and ENTER by one cycle. CODE words don't use the value in W, so they gain nothing from the autoincrement. The speed gained or lost is determined by the mix of Forth words executed. The usual rule is that most of the words executed are CODE words, thus, incrementing W in NEXT costs a bit of speed overall. (There is a memory savings, but DOCON, DOVAR, and ENTER appear only once, making this gain slight.)

The best decision, of course, depends upon the processor. On machines like the Z80, which only access memory by bytes and don't have autoincrement address modes, it is often best to leave W pointing to IP+1 (the last byte fetched from the Code Field). On other machines, autoincrementing is "free," and leaving W pointing to the Parameter Field is most convienient.

Remember: the decision must be made consistently. If NEXT leaves W pointing to the PFA of the word being executed, then EXECUTE must do likewise! (This was the 'oops' that I corrected at the start of this article.)

Direct Threading

Direct Threading works just like Indirect Threading, except that instead of the Code Field containing the address of some machine code, it contains a JUMP or CALL to some machine code. This makes the Code Field larger -- e.g., 1 byte larger in the 6809 -- but removes one level of indirection from the NEXT routine.

The choice of a JUMP or a CALL instruction in the Code Field hinges upon how the Parameter Field Address can be obtained by the machine code routine. In order to jump to the Code Field, many CPUs require that its address be in a register. For instance, the indirect jump on the 8086 is JMP AX (or some other register), and on the Z80 is JP (HL) (or IX or IY). On these processors, the DTC NEXT involves two operations, which on the 6809 would be:

NEXT:	LDX ,Y++	; (IP) -> W, and IP+2 -> IP
	JMP ,X	; JMP (W)

(On the 8086, this can be done with LODSW, JMP AX.) The effect of this is illustrated in Figure 4 as "case 1". The Code Field Address of DEUX is fetched from the high-level thread, and IP is incremented. Then, instead of a fetch, a JUMP is made to the Code Field Address (i.e., the CPU jumps directly to the Code Field). The CFA is left in the W register, just like the first ITC example above. Since this address is already in a register, we can simply put a JUMP to DOCON in the Code Field, and the DOCON fragment will work the same as before.

FIGURE 4. DTC BEFORE AND AFTER "NEXT"

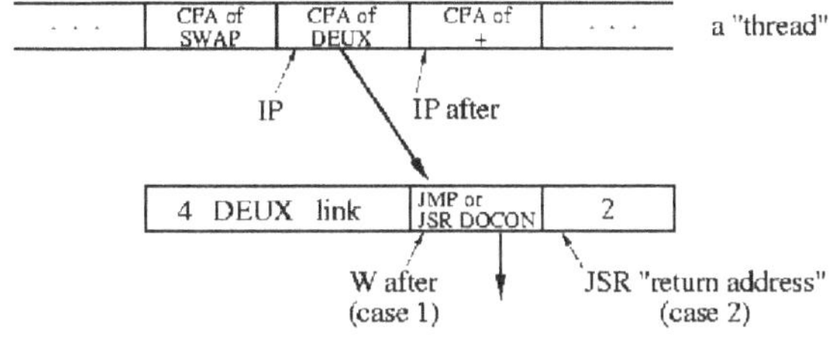

However, some processors -- such as the 6809 and PDP-11 -- can do this DTC NEXT in <u>one</u> instruction:

NEXT:	JMP [,Y++]	; (IP) -> temp, IP+2 -> IP, JMP (temp)

This, too, will cause the CPU to jump to the Code Field of DEUX. But there's one big difference: the CFA is not left in any register! So how is the machine code fragment to find the Parameter Field Address? By putting a CALL (JSR) in the Code Field instead of a JUMP. On most CPUs, the CALL instruction will push the return address -- the address immediately following the CALL instruction -- onto the Return Stack. As Figure 4 illustrates ("case 2"), this return address is exactly the Parameter Field Address we want! So, all DOCON has to do is pop the Return Stack -- balancing the JSR in the Code Field -- and then use that address to fetch the constant value. Thus:

DOCON:	PULS X	; pop the PFA from the Return Stack
	LDD ,X	; fetch the Parameter Field cell
	PSHU D	; push that on the Parameter Stack
	NEXT	; (macro) do the next high-level word

Compare this with the ITC version. One instruction has been added to DOCON, but one instruction has been deleted from NEXT. DOVAR and NEXT likewise become one instruction longer:

DOVAR:	PULS X	; pop the PFA of the word
	PSHU X	; push that address on the Parameter Stack
	NEXT	

ENTER:	PULS X	; pop the PFA of the word
	PSHS Y	; push the old IP
	TFR X,Y	; the PFA becomes the new IP
	NEXT	

Now go back to the beginning of this article, and reread my "oops," to see why we can't just re-fetch the CFA by using the IP. Also note the difference when the assignment of Forth's stack pointers to the 6809's U and S is reversed.

Subroutine Threading

Subroutine Threading (STC) is like DTC in that the CPU jumps directly to the Code Field of a Forth word. Only now there is no NEXT code, no IP register, and no W register. So, there is no choice but to use a JSR in the Code Field, since this is the only way to obtain the Parameter Field Address. This process is illustrated in Figure 5.

FIGURE 5. SUBROUTINE THREADED CODE

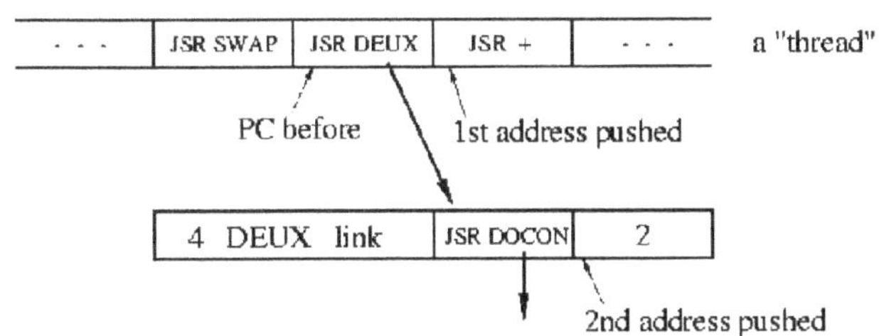

The high-level "thread" is a series of subroutine calls being executed by the CPU. When the JSR DEUX is executed, the address of the next instruction in the thread is pushed onto the Return Stack. Then, the JSR DOCON within the word DEUX is executed, which causes another return address -- the PFA of DEUX -- to be pushed onto the Return Stack. DOCON can pop that address, use it to fetch the constant, stack the constant, and then do an RTS to return to the thread:

DOCON:	PULS X	; pop the PFA from the Return Stack
	LDD ,X	; fetch the Parameter Field cell
	PSHU D	; push that on the Parameter Stack
	RTS	; do the next high-level word

We can still speak of a Code Field and a Parameter Field in Subroutine-Threaded Code. In every "class" of Forth word except CODE and colon defintions, the Code Field is the space occupied by a JSR or CALL instruction (just like DTC), and the Parameter Field is what follows. So, on the 6809, the PFA would equal CFA+3. The meaning of "Parameter Field" becomes somewhat fuzzy in CODE and colon definitions, as will be seen in future articles.

THE SPECIAL CASE: CODE WORDS

There is a significant exception to all of the above generalizations. This is CODE definitions -- Forth words that are defined as a machine code subroutine. This wonderful capability is trivially easy to implement in Forth, since every Forth word executes some piece of machine code!

The machine code comprising a CODE word is always contained in the body of the Forth word. In an Indirect-Threaded Forth, the Code Field must contain the address of the machine code to be executed. So the machine code is placed in the Parameter Field, and the Code Field contains the address of the Parameter Field, as shown in Figure 6.

FIGURE 6. CODE WORDS

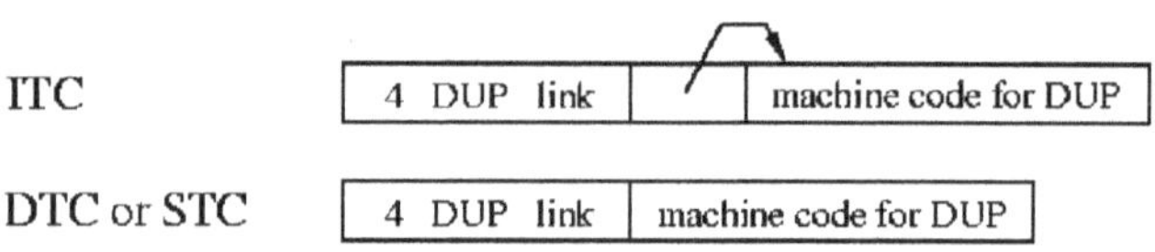

In Direct- and Subroutine-Threaded Forths, we could -- by analogy -- put, in the Code Field, a JUMP to the Parameter Field. But this would be pointless, since the Parameter Field immediately follows the Code Field! The Code Field could be filled with NOPs for the same result. Better still, the machine code could be started at the Code Field, and continued into the Parameter Field. At this point the distinction of "Code Field" and "Parameter Field" breaks down. This is no problem, because we don't need this distinction for CODE words. (This does have ramifications for decompilers and certain clever programming tricks, none of which concern us here.)
CODE words -- whatever the implementation -- are the one case where the machine code "action" routine does <u>not</u> need to be passed the Parameter Field address. The Parameter Field contains, not data, but the code being executed! Only NEXT needs to know this address (or the Code Field Address), so it can jump to the machine code.

USING ;CODE

Three questions remain unanswered:
a. how do we create a new Forth word that has some arbitrary data in its Parameter Field?
b. how do we change the Code Field of that word, to point to some machine code of our choosing?
c. how do we compile (assemble) this machine code fragment, which exists in isolation from the words using it?
The answer to (a) is: we write a Forth word to do this. Since this word, when executed, will define (create) a new word in the Forth dictionary, it is called a "defining word." CONSTANT is one example of a defining word. All of the "hard work" of a defining word is done by a kernel word, CREATE, which parses a name from the input stream, builds the header and Code Field for a new word, and links it into the dictionary. (In fig-Forth this word is called <BUILDS.) All that remains for the programmer is to build the Parameter Field.

The answer to (b) and (c) is embodied in two convoluted words called (;CODE) and ;CODE respectively. To understand how they work, let's look at how the defining word CONSTANT is actually written in Forth. Using the original ITC 6809 example:

: CONSTANT (n --)	
CREATE	**\ create the new word**
,	**\ append the TOS value to the dictionary,** **\ as the 1st cell of the Parameter Field**
;CODE	**\ end high-level & start assembler code**
LDD 2,X	**\ the code fragment DOCON**
PSHU D	**\ " " " "**
NEXT	**\ " " " "**
END-CODE	

There are two parts to this Forth word. Everything from **: CONSTANT** to **;CODE** is the high-level Forth code executed when the word CONSTANT is invoked. Everything from **;CODE** to **END-CODE** is machine code executed when the "children" of CONSTANT -- the "constant-class" words such as UN and DEUX -- are executed. That is, everything from ;CODE to END-CODE is the code fragment to which constant-type words will point. The name ;CODE signifies that it ends a high-level definition (";") and begins a machine- code definition ("CODE"). However, this is not put into the dictionary as two separate words. Everything from **: CONSTANT** to **END-CODE** is contained in the Parameter Field of CONSTANT, as shown in Figure 7.

FIGURE 7. ITC ;CODE

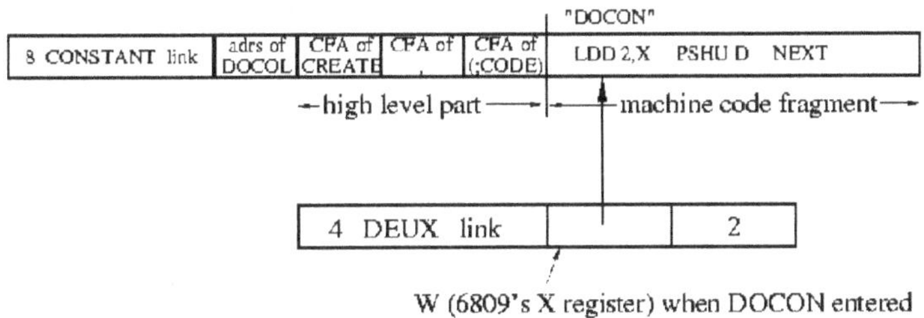

Derick and Baker [DER82] name three "sequences" that help to understand the action of defining words:

Sequence 1 is when the word CONSTANT is being defined. This involves both the high-level compiler (for the first part) and the Forth assembler (for the second part). This is when the definition of CONSTANT shown in Figure 7 is added to the dictionary. As we will see shortly, ;CODE -- a compiler directive -- is executed during Sequence 1.

Sequence 2 is when the word CONSTANT is being executed, and when some constant-type word is being defined. In the example

2 CONSTANT DEUX

Sequence 2 is when the word CONSTANT executes, and the word DEUX is added to the dictionary (as shown in Figure 7). During Sequence 2, the high-level part of CONSTANT is executed, including the word (;CODE).

Sequence 3 is when the constant-type word is executed. In our example, Sequence 3 is when DEUX is executed to push the value 2 onto the stack. This is when the machine-code part of CONSTANT is executed. (Recall that this fragment is the Code Field action of DEUX.)

The words ;CODE and (;CODE) do the following:

;CODE is executed during Sequence 1, when CONSTANT is compiled. This is an example of a Forth IMMEDIATE word -- a word executed during the Forth compilation. ;CODE does three things:

a. it compiles the Forth word (;CODE) into CONSTANT,
b. it turns off the Forth compiler, and
c. it turns on the Forth assembler.

(;CODE) is part of the word CONSTANT, so it executes when CONSTANT executes (Sequence 2). It performs the following actions:

a. It gets the address of the machine code that immediately follows. This is done by popping IP from the Forth Return Stack.
b. It puts that address into the Code Field of the word just defined by CREATE. The Forth word LAST (sometimes LATEST) gets the address of that word.
c. It does the action of EXIT (a.k.a. ;S) so that the Forth inner interpreter doesn't try to execute the machine code that follows as part of the Forth thread. This is the high-level "subroutine return" which ends a Forth thread.

F83 [LAX84] illustrates how these are typically coded in Forth:

: ;CODE	
COMPILE (;CODE)	**\ compiles (;CODE) into definition**
?CSP [COMPILE] [	**\ turns off the Forth compiler**
REVEAL	**\ (just like ";" does)**
ASSEMBLER	**\ turns on the assembler**
; IMMEDIATE	**\ this is an IMMEDIATE word!**

: (;CODE)	
R>	\ pops the adrs of the machine code
LAST @ NAME>	\ gets the CFA of the latest word
!	\ stores the code address in the
;	\ Code Field

(;CODE) is the more subtle of the two. Since it is a high-level Forth definition, the address following it in the CONSTANT thread -- the high-level "return address" -- is pushed onto Forth's Return Stack. So, popping the Return Stack while within (;CODE) will yield the address of the machine code that follows. Also, popping this value from the Return Stack will "bypass" one level of high-level subroutine return, so that when (;CODE) exits, it will exit to the caller of CONSTANT. This is equivalent to returning to CONSTANT, and then having CONSTANT return immediately. Use Figure 7 and walk through the execution of the words CONSTANT and (;CODE) to see how this works.

Direct and Subroutine Threading

For DTC and STC, the action of ;CODE and (;CODE) is identical to ITC, with one important exception: instead of holding an address, the Code Field holds a JUMP or CALL instruction. For an absolute JUMP or CALL, probably the only difference is that the address has to be stored at the end of the Code Field, as the operand of the JUMP or CALL instruction. In the case of the 6809, the address would be stored as the last two bytes of the three-byte JSR instruction. But some Forths, such as Pygmy Forth on the 8086, use a relative branch in the code field. In this case, the relative offset must be computed and inserted into the branch instruction.

HIGH-LEVEL FORTH ACTIONS

We have seen how to make a Forth word execute a chosen fragment of machine language code, and how to pass that fragment the address of the word's Parameter Field. But how do we write the "action routine" in high-level Forth?

Every Forth word must -- by the action of NEXT -- execute some machine language routine. This is what the Code Field is all about. Therefore, a machine language routine, or a set of routines, is needed to handle the problems of invoking a high- level action. We'll call this routine DODOES. There are three problems to be solved:

a. how do we find the address of the high-level action routine associated with this Forth word?

b. how do we, from machine code, invoke the Forth interpreter for a high-level action routine?

c. how do we pass that routine the address of the Parameter Field for the word we are executing?

The answer to (c) -- how do you pass an argument to a high-level Forth routine -- is easy. On the Parameter Stack, of course. Our machine language routine must push the Parameter Field Address on the stack before it invokes the high level routine. (From our previous work, we know how the machine language routine can obtain the PFA.)

The answer to (b) is a bit more difficult. Basically, we want to do something like the Forth word EXECUTE, which invokes a Forth word; or perhaps ENTER, which invokes a colon definition. Both are among our "key" kernel words. The DODOES code will resemble these.

Question (a) is the tricky one. Where to put the address of the high-level routine? Remember, the Code Field does not point to high-level code; it must point to machine code. Two approaches have been used in the past:

1. **The fig-Forth solution.** Fig-Forth reserved the first cell of the Parameter Field to hold the address of the high-level code. The DODOES routine then obtained the Parameter Field address, pushed the address of the actual data (typically PFA+2) onto the stack, fetched the address of the high-level routine, and EXECUTEd.

There were two problems with this approach. First, the structure of the Parameter Field was different for machine- code actions and high-level actions. For example, a CONSTANT defined with a machine code action would have its data stored at PFA, but a CONSTANT defined with a high-level action would have its data stored at (typically) PFA+2.

Second, every instance of a high-level-action class carried an additional overhead of one cell. That is, if CONSTANT used a high-level action, every constant defined in the program was one cell larger!

Fortunately, clever Forth programmers quickly devised a solution which overcame these problems, and the fig-Forth approach has fallen into disuse.

2. **The modern solution.** Most Forths nowadays associate a different machine language fragment with each high-level action routine. So, a high-level constant would have its Code Field pointing to a machine language fragment whose sole function is to invoke the high-level action of CONSTANT. A high-level variable's Code Field would point to the "startup" routine for the high-level VARIABLE action, and so on.

Is this excessive duplication of code? No, because each of these machine-language fragments is just a subroutine call to a common startup routine, DODOES. (This is different from the fig-Forth DODOES routine.) The address of the high-level code to DODOES is passed as an "inline" subroutine parameter. That is, the address of the high-level code is put immediately after the JSR/CALL instruction. DODOES can then pop the CPU stack and do a fetch to obtain this address.

Actually, we make two more simplifications. The high-level code itself is put immediately after the JSR/CALL instruction. Then DODOES pops the CPU stack, and obtains this address directly. And since we know this is high-level Forth code, we dispense with its Code Field and just compile the high-level thread...essentially incorporating the action of ENTER into DODOES.

Now each "defined" word just points to a bit of machine code...no space is consumed in its Parameter Field. This bit of machine code is a JSR or CALL instruction, followed by the high-level action routine. In the 6809 example, we have traded two bytes in every constant for a three-byte JSR that appears only once.

This is undoubtedly the most convoluted program logic in the entire Forth kernel! So, let's see how this is implemented in practice, using our trusty ITC 6809 example.

FIGURE 8. ITC DODOES

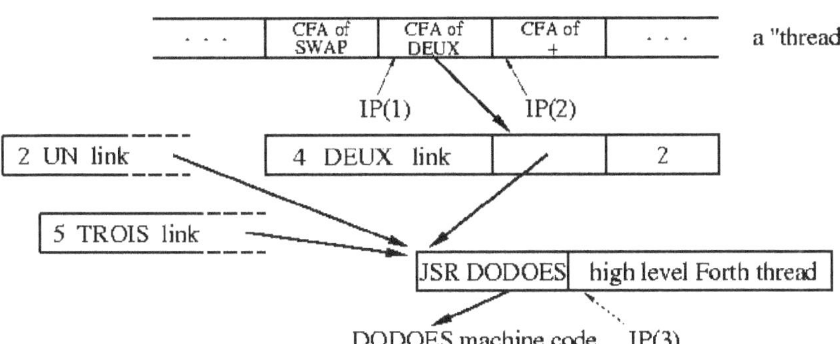

Figure 8 shows the constant DEUX implemented with a high-level action. When the Forth interpreter encounters DEUX -- that is, when the Forth IP is at IP(1) -- it does the usual thing: it fetches the address contained in DEUX's Code Field, and jumps to that address. At that address is a JSR DODOES instruction, so a second jump -- this time a subroutine call -- is immediately taken. DODOES must then perform the following actions:

a. Push the address of DEUX's Parameter Field onto the Parameter Stack, for later use by the high-level action routine. Since the JSR instruction does not alter any registers, we expect to find the Parameter Field Address of DEUX (or a "nearby" address) still in the W register.

b. Obtain the address of the high-level action routine, by popping the CPU stack. (Recall that popping the CPU stack will give the address of whatever immediately follows the JSR instruction.) This is a high-level thread, i.e., the Parameter Field part of a colon definition.

c. Save the old value of Forth's Instruction Pointer -- IP(2) -- on Forth's Return Stack, since the IP register will be used to execute the high-level fragment. Essentially, DODOES must "nest" the IP, just like ENTER does. Remember that Forth's Return Stack may not be the same as the CPU subroutine stack.

d. Put the address of the high-level thread into IP. This is IP(3) in Figure 8.

e. Do a NEXT to continue high-level interpretation at the new location.

Assume an indirect-threaded ITC 6809, and the following:

* W is not incremented by NEXT (i.e., W will contain the CFA of the word entered by NEXT);

* the 6809 S is Forth's PSP, and U is Forth's RSP (i.e., the CPU stack is not Forth's Return Stack);

* the 6809 Y is Forth's IP, and X is Forth's W.

Recall the definition of NEXT for these conditions:

NEXT:	LDX ,Y++	; (IP) -> W, and IP+2 -> IP
	JMP [,X]	; (W) -> temp, JMP (temp)

DODOES can be written as follows:

DODOES:	LEAX 2,X	; make W point to the Parameter Field
	PSHU Y	; (c) push old IP onto the Return Stack
	PULS Y	; (b,d) pop new IP from the CPU stack
	PSHS X	; (a) push W (the Parameter Field
		; Address) onto the Parameter Stack
	NEXT	; (e) invoke high-level interpreter

These operations are slightly out of sequence. As long as the right things go onto the right stacks (or into the right registers) at the right time, the exact order of operations is not critical. In this case, we're taking advantage of the fact that the old IP can be pushed onto Forth's Return Stack before the new IP is popped from the CPU stack.

On some processors the CPU stack is used as Forth's Return Stack. In this case, one step involving temporary storage is necessary. If we had chosen S=RSP and U=PSP above, DODOES would be:

DODOES:	LEAX 2,X	; make W point to the Parameter Field
	PSHU X	; (a) push W (the Parameter Field
		; Address) onto the Parameter Stack

	PULS X	**; (b) pop thread address from CPU stack**
	PSHS Y	**; (c) push old IP onto the Return Stack**
	TFR X,Y	**; (d) put thread address into IP**
	NEXT	**; (e) invoke high-level interpreter**

Since we are essentially swapping the top of the Return/CPU stack with IP, we need to use X as a temporary holding register. Thus we must push the PFA -- step (a) -- before re-using the X register.

Walk through both of these DODOES examples step by step, and track the contents of the registers and the two stacks. I always walk through my DODOES routine, just to make sure I'm not clobbering a register at the wrong time.

Direct Threading

The logic of DODOES is the same in DTC Forths. But the implementation may be different, depending on whether the DTC Forth uses a JMP or a CALL in the Code Field of a word.

a. **JMP in Code Field.** A DTC Forth can use a JMP in the Code Field if the address of the word being executed is found in a register. This will most likely be the Code Field Address.

From the point of view of DODOES, this is identical to ITC. In our example, DODOES sees that the Forth interpreter jumps to the machine code associated with DEUX, and that code is a JSR to DODOES. It doesn't matter that the first jump is now a direct jump rather than an indirect jump; the register and stack contents are the same. So, the code for DODOES will be identical to that for ITC. (Of course, NEXT is different, and W may need a different offset to point to the Parameter Field.)

b. **CALL/JSR in Code Field.** In the DTC 6809, we never explicitly fetch the CFA of the word being executed, so the Forth word must contain a JSR in its Code Field. Instead of finding the Parameter Field Address of the Forth word in a register, we find it on the CPU stack.

FIGURE 9. DTC DODOES

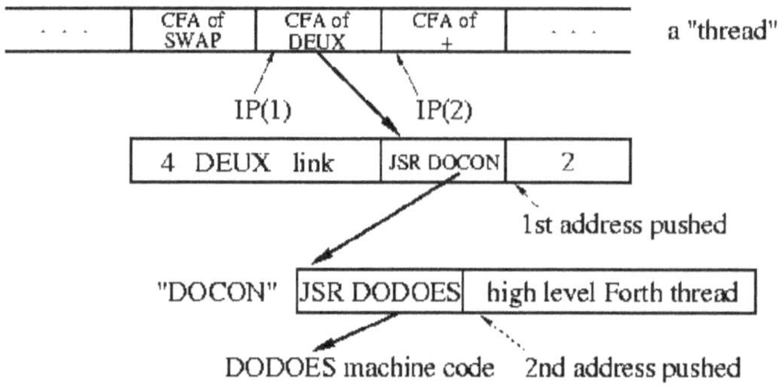

. . . | CFA of SWAP | CFA of DEUX | CFA of + | . . . a "thread"

IP(1) IP(2)

4 DEUX link | JSR DOCON | 2

1st address pushed

"DOCON" | JSR DODOES | high level Forth thread

DODOES machine code 2nd address pushed

The DEUX example in this case is shown in Figure 9. When the Forth IP is at IP(1), the Forth interpreter jumps to the Code Field of DEUX (and increments IP). In the Code Field is a JSR to DEUX's machine code fragment. At that address is a second JSR, to DODOES. So two things get pushed onto the CPU stack. The return address of the first JSR is the Parameter Field address of DEUX.

The return address of the second JSR -- and thus topmost on the CPU stack -- is the address of the high- level thread to be executed. DODOES must ensure that the old IP is pushed onto the Return Stack, the PFA of DEUX is pushed onto the Parameter Stack, and the address of the high-level thread is loaded into IP. This is very sensitive to stack assignments! For S=PSP (CPU stack) and U=RSP, the NEXT and DODOES code is:

NEXT:	**LDX [,Y++]**	**; (IP) -> temp, IP+2 -> IP, JMP (temp)**
DODOES:	**PSHU Y**	**; push old IP onto the Return Stack**
	PULS Y	**; pop new IP from the CPU stack**
		; note: the CPU stack is the
		; Parameter Stack, and the
		; topmost element is now the PFA of
		; the word exactly what we want!
	NEXT	**; invoke high-level interpreter**

Check for yourself that the flow through NEXT, DEUX, and DODOES pushes a net total of one item -- the PFA of DEUX -- onto the Parameter Stack!

Subroutine Threading

In STC Forths, there are no IP or W registers, and a high-level "thread" is pure machine code (a series of subroutine calls). The only difference between a high-level action and a ;CODE action is that the PFA of the "defined" word must be pushed onto the Parameter Stack. "Defined" words have a CALL/JSR in the Code Field, and the CPU stack must be Forth's Return Stack, so DODOES is mostly a matter of stack manipulations.

FIGURE 10. STC DODOES

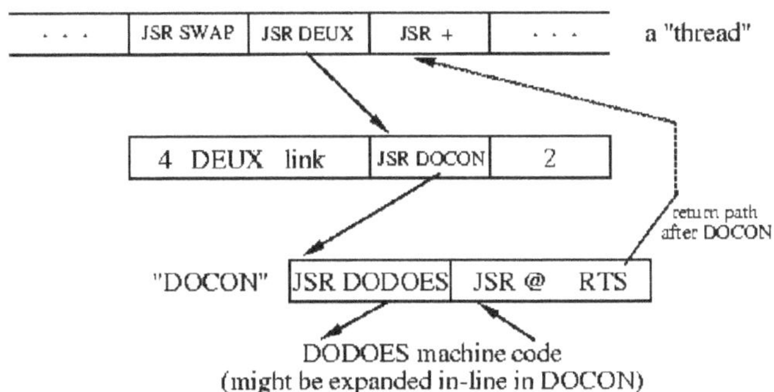

Figure 10 shows a 6809 STC example of DEUX with a high-level action. By the time DODOES is entered, three things have been pushed onto the CPU/Return Stack: the return address in the "main" thread, the PFA of DEUX, and the address of DEUX's high- level action code. DODOES must pop the last two, push the PFA onto the Parameter Stack, and jump to the action code:

DODOES:	PULS X,Y	; action code adrs -> X, PFA -> Y
	PSHU Y	; push PFA onto Parameter Stack
	JMP ,X	; jump to the action code

DODOES for the 6809 is now a three-instruction routine. It can be simplified even further by "expanding JSR DODOES in-line," i.e., replacing the JSR DODOES with the equivalent machine code instructions. Since there's one less JSR, this simplifies the stack manipulation to:

	PULS X	; pop PFA from CPU stack
	PSHU X	; and push it onto the Parameter Stack
		; ...high level thread for DEUX...

This replaces a three-byte JSR with four bytes of explicit code, with a considerable improvement in speed. For the 6809 this would probably be a good choice. For a processor like the 8051, DODOES is long enough that it should be kept as a subroutine.

USING DOES>

We learned with ;CODE how to create a new Forth word with arbitrary data in its parameter field, and how to make that word's Code Field point to a new machine code fragment. How do we compile a high-level action routine, and make a new word point to it?

The answer lies in the two words DOES> and (DOES>), which are the high-level equivalents of ;CODE and (;CODE). To understand them, let's look at an example of their use:

: CONSTANT (n --)	
CREATE	**\ create the new word**
,	**\ append the TOS value to the dictionary,**
	\ as the 1st cell of the Parameter Field
DOES>	**\ end "create" part & start "action" part**
@	**\ given the PFA, fetch its contents**
;	

Compare this with the previous ;CODE example, and observe that DOES> performs a function analogous to ;CODE. Everything from **: CONSTANT** to **DOES>** is executed when the word CONSTANT is invoked. This is the code which builds the Parameter Field of the "defined" word.

Everything from **DOES>** to ; is the high-level code executed when the "children" of CONSTANT (such as DEUX) are invoked, i.e., the high-level fragment to which the Code Field will point. (We'll see that a JSR DODOES is included before this high-level fragment.) Just as with ;CODE, both the "create" and the "action" clauses are contained within the body of the Forth word CONSTANT, as shown in Figure 11.

FIGURE 11. ITC DOES>

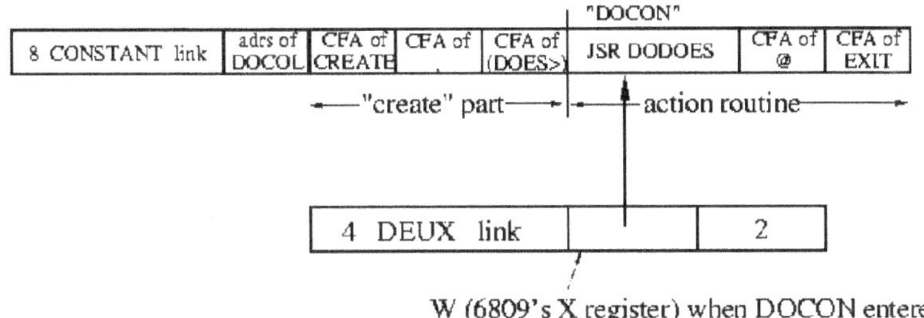

Recall Sequence 1, 2, and 3. The words DOES> and (DOES>) do the following:
DOES> is executed during Sequence 1, when CONSTANT is compiled. Thus DOES> is a Forth IMMEDIATE word. It does two things:

a. It compiles the Forth word (DOES>) into CONSTANT.
b. It compiles a JSR DODOES into CONSTANT.

Note that DOES> leaves the Forth compiler running, in order to compile the high-level fragment which follows. Also, even though JSR DODOES is not itself Forth code, an IMMEDIATE word such as DOES> can cause it to be compiled in the middle of Forth code.
(DOES>) is part of the word CONSTANT, so it executes when CONSTANT executes (Sequence 2). It does the following:

a. It gets the address of the machine code that immediately follows (JSR DODOES), by popping IP from the Forth Return Stack.
b. It puts that address into the Code Field of the word just defined by CREATE.
c. It performs the action of EXIT, causing CONSTANT to terminate here and not attempt to execute the fragment that follows.

The action of (DOES>) is identical to (;CODE)! A separate word is not strictly required. F83, for example, uses (;CODE) in both ;CODE and DOES>. I'll use (;CODE) from now on instead of (DOES>).
You've already seen the workings of (;CODE). The F83 definition of DOES> is

: DOES>	
COMPILE (;CODE)	**\ compiles (;CODE) into definition**
0E8 C,	**\ the CALL opcode byte**
DODOES HERE 2+ - ,	**\ the relative offset to DODOES**
; IMMEDIATE	

where DODOES is a constant which holds the address of the DODOES routine. (The actual F83 source code is slightly different, due to the requirements of the F83 metacompiler.) DOES> need not fiddle with CSP or the smudge bit, since the Forth compiler is left "on." In the case of the 8086, the CALL instruction expects a relative address...hence the arithmetic involving DODOES and HERE. In the 6809, DOES> would look like

: DOES>	
COMPILE (;CODE)	**\ compiles (;CODE) into definition**
0BD C,	**\ the JSR Extended opcode byte**
DODOES ,	**\ the operand: address of DODOES**
; IMMEDIATE	

You can see here how the machine language JSR DODOES is compiled after the high-level (;CODE), and before the high-level "action" code.

Direct and Subroutine Threading

The only difference in DTC and STC is how the Code Field is fiddled to point to a new routine. This is done by (;CODE), and the required changes have already been described. DOES> isn't affected at all, unless you're writing an STC Forth and expanding the JSR DODOES to explicit machine code. In this case, DOES> is modified to assemble the "in-line" machine code instead of a JSR DODOES instruction.

ONWARD AND UPWARD

Who would have thought that so few lines of code would require so much explanation? This is why I admire ;CODE and DOES> so much...I've never before seen seen such intricate, powerful, and flexible constructs coded with such economy.

In the next installment I'll discuss the merits of assemblers vs. metacompilers, and provide the actual CODE definitions for our Forth example systems.

REFERENCES

[DER82] Derick, Mitch and Baker, Linda, Forth Encyclopedia, Mountain View Press (1982). A word-by-word description of fig- Forth in minute detail. Still available from the Forth Interest Group, P.O. Box 2154, Oakland CA 94621.

[LAX84] Laxen, H. and Perry, M., F83 for the IBM PC, version 2.1.0 (1984). Distributed by the authors, available from the Forth Interest Group or GEnie.

Author's note for web publication: the files formerly available on the GEnie online service are now available from the Forth Interest Group FTP server, ftp://ftp.forth.org/pub/Forth.

Continue with Part 4 | Back to publications page

MOVING FORTH by Brad Rodriguez

Part 4: Assemble or Metacompile?

This article first appeared in **The Computer Journal** #64 (November/December 1993).

"Keep it SHORT!" was the editorial directive for this installment. So I apologize for postponing the source listings to yet another issue. In the meantime, there is a new decision to contemplate:

How do you build a Forth system for the Very First Time?

You know now that most Forth code is high-level "threads," usually compiled as just a series of addresses. In the early days of fig-Forth, assemblers were often the only programming tools available. This was fine for writing Forth CODE words, but high- level threads had to be written as a series of DW directives. For example, the Forth word

```
: MAX ( n n - n)  OVER OVER < IF SWAP THEN DROP ;
```

would be written [TAL80]

	DW OVER,OVER,LESS,ZBRAN
	DW MAX2-$
	DW SWAP
MAX2:	**DW DROP,SEMIS**

Later, as working Forth systems became widespread, Forthwrights began modifying the Forth compilers into cross-compilers [CAS80]. Thus with Forth on your CP/M machine (or Apple II, or whatever), you could write Forth programs for some other CPU...up to and including an entirely new Forth system for that CPU.

Because they create a new Forth from within Forth, these are often called metacompilers. Computer science purists object to this, so some Forthies use the terms "cross-compiler" and "recompiler." The difference is that a recompiler can only generate a new Forth for the <u>same</u> CPU.

Most PC Forths are now produced with metacompilers, but opinion is divided in the embedded systems arena [TIN91,ROD91,SER91]. The arguments for using assemblers to write Forth are:

1. Metacompilers are cryptic and hard to understand, and you must thoroughly understand a metacompiler in order to use it.
2. Assemblers are understood by the average programmer.
3. An assembler is almost always available for a new CPU.
4. Assemblers handle many optimizations (e.g. short vs. long branch).
5. Assemblers handle forward references and peculiar address modes; many metacompilers don't.
6. Assemblers use familiar editing and debugging tools.
7. The code generation is completely visible -- nothing is "hidden" from the programmer.
8. It's easier to tweak the Forth model, since many design decisions affect the internals of a metacompiler.

The arguments for metacompilers:

1. You write "normal" looking Forth code, which is easier to read and debug.
2. Once you understand your metacompiler, you can port it easily to new CPUs.
3. The only tool you need to acquire is a Forth for your computer.

The last is particularly applicable to those who don't own PCs, since most cross-assemblers require PCs or workstations these days.
I've written several Forths each way, so I'm painfully aware of the tradeoffs. I admit a preference for metacompilers: I find the Forth code for MAX much easier to read and understand than its assembler equivalent. Most of the arguments against metacompilers have been overcome by modern "professional" compilers, and if you're using Forth for work I strongly recommend investing in a commercial product. Alas, public-domain metacompilers (including my own) are still behind the times, clunky, and arcane.

So I'm going to take a radical position for a Forth programmer, and tell you to choose for yourself. I'll publish the 6809 code in metacompiler form, and I'll supply a metacompiler for F83 (IBM PC, CP/M, or Atari ST) [ROD92]. The Z80 code will be written for a CP/M assembler. The 8051 code will be written for a public- domain PC cross-assembler.

Forth in C?

No discussion of this topic would be complete without mentioning a new trend: Forths written in C. These have the advantage of being more portable than assembler -- in theory, all you have to do is recompile the same source code for any CPU. The disadvantages:

1. Less flexibility in the design decisions; e.g., direct-threaded code is probably not possible, and you can't optimize register assignments.
2. You have to recompile the C source to add new primitives.
3. Forth words carry the C call-and-return overhead.
4. Some C Forths use inefficient threading techniques, e.g. a CASE statement.
5. Most C compilers produce less efficient code than a good assembly-language programmer.

But for Unix systems and RISC workstations, which frown upon assembler, this may be the only way to get a Forth up and running. The most complete and widely used of the public-domain C Forths *[at the time of publication]* is TILE (TILE_21.ZIP, file #2263 on GEnie's Forth Roundtable). If you're not running Unix, you should look instead at the Genie files HENCE4TH_1.2.A (#2490) and CFORTHU.ARC (#2079).
To continue the previous comparison, here's the definition of MAX from HENCE4TH [MIS90]. I omit the dictionary headers for clarity:

```
        DW OVER,OVER,LESS,ZBRAN
```

```
    _max() {
        OVER OVER LESS IF SWAP ENDIF DROP }
```

Instead of assembler, C is used to write the CODE words in the kernel. For example, here is HENCE4TH's SWAP:

_swap() {	
register cell i = *(dsp);	
*(dsp) = *(dsp + 1);	
*(dsp + 1) = i;	
}	

(Please note: there is quite a variety of techniques for writing Forth words in C, so these words may appear radically different in CFORTH or TILE.)

On a 68000 or SPARC, this might produce quite good code. On a Z80 or 8051, quite the opposite. But even if you plan to write a Forth in C, you need to understand how Forth works in assembler. So stay tuned for the next installment of Moving Forth!

REFERENCES

[CAS80] Cassady, John J., METAFORTH: A Metacompiler for Fig- Forth, Forth Interest Group (1980).

[MIS90] HenceFORTH in C, Version 1.2, distributed by The Missing Link, 975 East Ave. Suite 112, Chico, CA 95926, USA (1990). This is a shareware product available from the GEnie Forth Roundtable.

[ROD91] Rodriguez, B.J., letter to the editor, Forth Dimensions XIII:3 (Sep/Oct 1991), p.5.

[ROD92] Rodriguez, B.J., "Principles of Metacompilation," Forth Dimensions XIV:3 (Sep/Oct 1992), XIV:4 (Nov/Dec 1992), and XIV:5 (Jan/Feb 1993). Note that the published code is for a fig-Forth variant and not F83. The F83 version is on GEnie as CHROMIUM.ZIP

[SER91] Sergeant, Frank, "Metacompilation Made Easy," Forth Dimensions XII:6 (Mar/Apr 1991).

[TAL80] Talbot, R.J., fig-Forth for 6809, Forth Interest Group, P.O. Box 2154, Oakland, CA 94621 (1980).

[TIN91] Ting, C.H., "How Metacompilation Stops the Growth Rate of Forth Programmers," Forth Dimensions XIII:1 (May/Jun 1991), p.17.

Author's note for web publication: the files formerly available on the GEnie online service are now available from the Forth Interest Group FTP server, ftp://ftp.forth.org/pub/Forth.

Also, several new Forths-in-C have been published since this article was first written. Consult the "systems" FAQ at ftp://ftp.forth.org/pub/Forth/FAQ *for a current list.*

Continue with Part 5 Back to publications page

MOVING FORTH by Brad Rodriguez

Part 5: The Z80 Primitives

This article first appeared in **The Computer Journal** #67 (May/June 1994).

THE CODE I PROMISED

At long last, I am ready to present the complete source code for an (I hope) ANSI compliant Forth, CamelForth[1]. As an intellectual exercise -- and to ensure a clear copyright -- I've written this code entirely from scratch. (Do you know how hard it is to *not* look at excellent code examples?) Of course, my experience with various Forths has no doubt influenced some design decisions.

Due to space limitations, the source code will be presented in four installments (if you can't wait, complete files will be on GEnie):

1. Z80 Forth "primitives," in assembler source
2. 8051 Forth "primitives," likewise
3. Z80/8051 high-level kernel, likewise
4. complete 6809 kernel, in metacompiler source

For CamelForth I'm trying to use exclusively public-domain tools: for the Z80, the Z80MR assembler under CP/M [3]; for the 8051, the A51 cross-assembler on an IBM PC [4], and for the 6809, my own metacompiler under F83 for CP/M, IBM PC, or Atari ST.

By "kernel" I mean the set of words that comprises a basic Forth system, including compiler and interpreter. For CamelForth this is the ANS Forth Core word set, plus any non-ANSI words necessary to implement the Core word set. A Forth kernel is usually written partly in machine code (as CODE words), and partly in high-level Forth. The words which are written in machine code are called the "primitives," since, in the final analysis, the entire Forth system is defined in terms of just these words.

Exactly *which* words should be written in machine code? The selection of the optimal set of primitives is an interesting debate. A smaller set of primitives makes for easier porting, but poorer performance. I've been told that a set of 13 primitives is sufficient to define all of Forth -- a *very slow* Forth. eForth [2], designed for easy porting, had a more generous set of 31 primitives. My rules are these:

1. Fundamental arithmetic, logic, and memory operators are CODE.
2. If a word *can't* be easily or efficiently written (or written at all) in terms of other Forth words, it should be CODE (e.g., U<, RSHIFT).
3. If a simple word is used frequently, CODE may be worthwhile (e.g., NIP, TUCK).

4. If a word requires fewer bytes when written in CODE, do so (a rule I learned from Charles Curley).
5. If the processor includes instruction support for a word's function, put it in CODE (e.g. CMOVE or SCAN on a Z80 or 8086).
6. If a word juggles many parameters on the stack, but has relatively simple logic, it may be better in CODE, where the parameters can be kept in registers.
7. If the logic or control flow of a word is complex, it's probably better in high-level Forth.

For Z80 CamelForth I have a set of about 70 primitives. (See Table 1.) Having already decided on the Forth model and CPU usage (see my previous TCJ articles), I followed this development procedure:

1. Select the subset of the ANSI Core word set which will be primitives. (Subject to revision, of course.)
2. From the ANSI descriptions, write assembler definitions of these words, plus the processor initialization code.
3. Run this through the assembler, fixing source code errors.
4. Test that you can produce working machine code. I usually add a few lines of assembler code to output a character once the initialization is complete. This seemingly trivial test is crucial! It ensures that your hardware, assembler, "downloader" (EPROM emulator or whatever), and serial communications are all working!
5. (Embedded systems only.) Add another assembler code fragment to read the serial port and echo it back...thus testing *both* directions of communications.
6. Write a *high-level* Forth fragment to output a character, using *only* Forth primitives. (Usually something like "LIT,33h,EMIT,BYE".) This tests the Forth register initialization, the stacks, and the threading mechanism. Problems at this stage can usually be traced to logic errors in NEXT or in the initialization, or data stack goofs (e.g. stack in ROM).
7. Write a colon definition to output a character, and include it in the high-level fragment from step 6. (E.g., define BLIP as "LIT,34h,EMIT,EXIT" and then test the fragment "LIT,33h,EMIT, BLIP,BYE".) Problems at this stage are usually with DOCOLON or EXIT logic, or return stack goofs.
8. At this point you can write some tools to help you with debugging, such as words to display in hex a number on the stack. Listing 1 shows a simple test routine to do a never-ending memory dump (useful even if your keyboard doesn't work). This tests the primitives DUP, EMIT, EXIT, C@, ><, LIT, 1+, and BRANCH, as well as several levels of nesting. Plus, it doesn't use DO..LOOP, which are often

difficult to get working. When this code works, you have some confidence that your basic Forth model is valid.

9. From here on it's just testing the remaining primitives -- DO..LOOP, UM/MOD, UM*, and DODOES are particularly tricky -- and adding high-level definitions. I like to get a rudimentary interpreter going next, so that I can test words interactively.

With this set of primitives you can begin writing Forth code. Sure, you have to use an assembler instead of a Forth compiler, but -- as Listing 1 suggests -- you can use high-level control flow and nesting to write useful code that would be more difficult to write in assembler.

READ THE CODE!

I've run out of abstractions for today. If you want to learn more about how a Forth kernel works and is written, study Listing 2. It follows the Forth convention for documentation:

WORD-NAME stack in -- stack out description

WORD-NAME is the name by which *Forth* knows the word. Often these names include peculiar ASCII characters, so an approximation must be used when defining assembler labels (such as ONEPLUS for the Forth word 1+).
stack in are the arguments this word expects to see on the stack, with the topmost stack item always on the right. stack out are the arguments this word will leave on the stack, likewise.
If the word has a return stack effect (other than nesting, that is), an additional return stack comment will be added after "R:"

stack in -- stack out   R: stack in -- stack out

ANSI Forth defines a number of useful abbreviations for stack arguments, such as "n" for a signed single-cell number, "u" for an unsigned single-cell number, "c" for a character, and so on.
See Table 1.

REFERENCES

[1] **Definition of a camel:** a horse designed by committee.

[2] **Ting, C. H.,** eForth Implementation Guide, July 1990, available from Offete Enterprises, 1306 South B Stret, San Mateo, CA 94402 USA.

[3] Z80MR, a Z80 Macro Assembler by Mike Rubenstein, is public-domain, available on the GEnie CP/M Roundtable as file Z80MR-A.LBR. Warning: do *not* use the supplied Z1.COM program, use only Z80MR and LOAD. Z1 has a problem with conditional jumps.
[4] A51, PseudoCorp's freeware Level 1 cross-assembler for the 8051, is available from the Realtime and Control Forth Board, (303) 278-0364, or on the GEnie Forth Roundtable as file A51.ZIP. PseudoCorp's commercial products are advertised here in TCJ.

Source code for Z80 CamelForth is available on this site at http://www.camelforth.com/public_ftp/cam80-12.zip.
Continue with Part 6 | Back to publications page

MOVING FORTH by Brad Rodriguez

Part 6: The Z80 high-level kernel

This article first appeared in **The Computer Journal** #69 (September/October 1994).

ERRATA

There are two goofs in the CAMEL80.AZM file I presented in TCJ#67. The minor goof is that the name length specified in the HEAD macro for the Forth word > was incorrectly typed as 2 instead of 1.

The major goof results from a subtlety of CP/M console I/O. KEY must not echo the typed character, and so used BDOS function 6. KEY? used BDOS function 11 to test non-destructively for the presence of a keypress. Unfortunately, BDOS function 6 does not "clear" the keypress detected by function 11! I have now rewritten KEY? to use BDOS function 6 (see Listing 1). Since this is a "destructive" test, I had to add logic to save the "consumed" keypress and return it when KEY is next used. This new logic can be used whenever your hardware (or operating system) provides only a destructive test-for-keypress.

HIGH LEVEL DEFINITIONS

In the last installment I did not expound greatly on the source code. Each Forth "primitive" performs a miniscule, sharply-defined function. It was almost all Z80 assembler code, and if it wasn't obvious *why* a particular word was included, I hope it was clear *what* each word did.

In this installment I have no such luxury: I will present the high level definitions which embody the elegant (and tortuous) logic of the Forth language. Entire books have been written [1,2,3] describing Forth kernels, and if you want complete mastery I highly recommend you buy one of them. For TCJ I'll limit myself to some of the key words of the compiler and interpreter, given in Listing 2.

TEXT INTERPRETER OPERATION

The text or "outer" interpreter is the Forth code which accepts input from the keyboard and performs the desired Forth operations. (This is distinct from the address or "inner" interpreter, NEXT, which executes compiled threaded code.) The best way to understand it is to work through the startup of the Forth system.

1. The CP/M entry point (see listing in previous installment) determines the top of available memory, set the stack pointers (PSP,RSP) and user pointer (UP), establishing the memory map shown in Figure 1. It then sets the "inner" interpreter pointer (IP) to execute the Forth word **COLD**.

2. **COLD** initializes the user variables from a startup table, and then does **ABORT**. (**COLD** will also attempt to execute a Forth command from the CP/M command line.)

3. **ABORT** resets the parameter stack pointer and does **QUIT**.

4. **QUIT** resets the return stack pointer, loop stack pointer, and interpret state, and then begins to interpret Forth commands. (The name is apt because **QUIT** can be used to abort an application and get back to the "top level" of Forth. Unlike **ABORT**, **QUIT** will leave the parameter stack contents alone.) **QUIT** is an infinite loop which will **ACCEPT** a line from the keyboard, and then **INTERPRET** it as Forth commands. When not compiling, **QUIT** will prompt "ok" after each line.

5. **INTERPRET** is an almost verbatim translation of the algorithm given in section 3.4 of the ANS Forth document. It parses one space-delimited string from the input, and tries to **FIND** the Forth word of that name. If the word is found, it will be either executed (if it is an IMMEDIATE word, or if in the "interpret" state, STATE=0) or compiled into the dictionary (if in the "compile" state, STATE<>0). If not found, Forth attempts to convert the string as a number. If successful, **LITERAL** will either place it on the parameter stack (if in "interpret" state) or compile it as an in-line literal value (if in "compile" state). If not a Forth word and not a valid number, the string is typed, an error message is displayed, and the interpreter **ABORT**s. This process is repeated, string by string, until the end of the input line is reached.

THE FORTH DICTIONARY

Whoa! How does the interpreter "find" a Forth word by name? Answer: Forth keeps a "dictionary" of the names of all Forth words. Each name is connected in some fashion with the executable code for the corresponding word.

There are many ways to store a set of strings for searching: a simple array, a linked list, a multiple linked list, hash table, etc. Almost all are valid here -- all Forth asks is that, if you reuse a name, the *latest* definition is found when you search the dictionary. It's also possible to have several sets of names ("vocabularies", or "wordlists" in the new ANSI jargon). This lets you reuse a name *without* losing its previous meaning. For example, you could have an integer +, a floating-point +, even a + for strings...one way to achieve the "operator overloading" so beloved by the object-oriented community.

Each string may be connected with its executable code by being physically adjacent in memory -- i.e., the name appears in memory just before the executable code, thus being called the "head" or "header" of the Forth word. Or the strings may be located in a totally different part of memory, and connected with pointers to executable code ("separate heads").

You can even have unnamed ("headless") fragments of Forth code, if you *know* you'll never need to compile or interpret them. ANSI only requires that the ANS Forth words be findable.

The design decisions could fill another article. Suffice it to say that CamelForth uses the simplest scheme: a single linked list, with the header located just before the executable code. No vocabularies... although I may add them in a future issue of TCJ.

HEADER STRUCTURE (FIGURE 2)

Still more design decisions: what data should be present in the header, and how should it be stored?

The minimum data is the name, precedence bit, and pointer (explicit or implicit) to executable code. For simplicity, CamelForth stores the name as a "counted string" (one byte of length, followed by N characters). Early Forth Inc. products stored a length but only the first three characters, for faster comparisons (the actual improvement gained is another hot debate). Fig-Forth compromised, flagging the last character with MSB high in order to allow either full-length or truncated names. Other Forths have used packed strings [4], and I suspect even C-style null-terminated strings have been used.

The "precedence bit" is a flag which indicates if this word has IMMEDIATE status. IMMEDIATE words are executed *even during compilation*, which is how Forth implements compiler directives and control structres. There are other ways to distinguish compiler directives -- Pygmy Forth [5], for example, puts them in a separate vocabulary. But ANS Forth essentially mandates the use of a precedence bit [6]. Many Forths store this bit in the "length" byte. I have chosen to put it in a separate byte, in order to use the "normal" string operators on word names (e.g. **S=** within **FIND**, and **TYPE** within **WORDS**).

If the names are kept in a linked list, there must be a link. Usually the latest word is at the head of the linked list, and the link points to a previous word. This enforces the ANSI (and traditional) requirement for redefined words. Charles Curley [7] has studied the placement of the link field, and found that the compiler can be made significantly faster if the link field comes *before* the name (rather than after, as was done in Fig-Forth).

Figure 2 shows the structure of the CamelForth word header, and the Fig-Forth, F83, and Pygmy Forth headers for comparison. The "view" vield of F83 and Pygmy is an example of other useful information which can be stored in the Forth word header.

Remember: it's important to distinguish the header from the "body" (executable part) of the word. They need not be stored together. The header is only used during compilation and interpretation, and a "purely executable" Forth application could

dispense with headers entirely. However, headers must be present -- at least for the ANSI word set -- for it to be a legal ANS Forth System.
When "compiling" a Forth system from assembler source code, you can define macros to build this header (see HEAD and IMMED in CAMEL80.AZM). In the Forth environment the header, *and the Code Field*, is constructed by the word **CREATE**.

COMPILER OPERATION

We now know enough to understand the Forth compiler. The word : starts a new high-level definition, by creating a header for the word (**CREATE**), changing its Code Field to "docolon" (**!COLON**), and switching to compile state (**]**). Recall that, in compile state, every word encountered by the text interpreter is compiled into the dictionary instead of being executed. This will continue until the word ; is encountered. Being an IMMEDIATE word, ; will execute, compiling an **EXIT** to end the definition, and then switching back to interpret state (**[**).
Also, : will **HIDE** the new word, and ; will **REVEAL** it (by setting and clearing the "smudge" bit in the name). This is to allow a Forth word to be redefined in terms of its "prior self". To force a recursive call to the word being defined, use **RECURSE**.
Thus we see that there is no distinct Forth "compiler", in the same sense that we would speak of a C or Pascal compiler. The Forth compiler is embodied in the actions of various Forth words. This makes it easy for you to change or extend the compiler, but makes it difficult to create a Forth application *without* a built-in compiler!

THE DEPENDENCY WORD SET

Most of the remaining high-level words are either a) necessary to implement the compiler and interpreter, or b) provided solely for your programming pleasure. But there is one set which deserves special mention: the words I have separated into the file CAMEL80D.AZM (Listing 3).
One of the goals of the ANSI Forth Standard was to hide CPU and model dependencies (Direct or Indirect Threaded? 16 or 32 bit?) from the application programmer. Several words were added to the Standard for this purpose. I have taken this one step further, attempting to encapsulate these dependencies *even within the kernel*. Ideally, the high-level Forth code in the file CAMEL80H.AZM should be the same for all CamelForth targets (although different assemblers will have different syntax).
Differences in cell size and word alignment are managed by the ANS Forth words **ALIGN ALIGNED CELL+ CELLS CHAR+ CHARS** and my own addition, **CELL** (equivalent to **1 CELLS**, but smaller when compiled).
The words **COMPILE, !CF ,CF !COLON** and **,EXIT** hide peculiarities of the threading model, such as a) how are the threads represented, and b) how is the Code Field

implemented? The value of these words becomes evident when you look at the differences between the direct-threaded Z80 and the subroutine-threaded 8051:

word	compiles on Z80	compiles on 8051
COMPILE,	address	LCALL address
!CF	CALL address	LCALL address
,CF	!CF & allot	3 bytes !CF & allot 3 bytes
!COLON	CALL docolon	nothing!
,EXIT	address of EXIT	RET

(**!CF** and **,CF** are different for indirect-threaded Forths.)

In similar fashion, the words **,BRANCH ,DEST** and **!DEST** hide the implementation of high-level branch and loop operators. I have tried to invent -- without borrowing from existing Forths! -- the minimal set of operators which can factor out all the implementation differences. Only time, expert criticism, and many CamelForths will tell how successful I've been.

So far I have *not* been successful factoring the differences in header structure into a similar set of words. The words **FIND** and **CREATE** are so intimately involved with the header contents that I haven't yet found suitable subfactors. I have made a start, with the words **NFA>LFA NFA>CFA IMMED? HIDE REVEAL** and the ANS Forth words **>BODY IMMEDIATE**. I'll continue to work on this. Fortunately, it is practical for the time being to use the identical header structure on all CamelForth implementations (since they're all byte-addressed 16-bit Forths).

NEXT TIME...

I will probably present the 8051 kernel, and talk about how the Forth compiler and interpreter are modified for Harvard architectures (computers that have logically distinct memories for Code and Data, like the 8051). For the 8051 I will print the files CAMEL51 and CAMEL51D, but probably only excerpts from CAMEL51H, since (except for formatting of the assembler file) the high-level code shouldn't be different from what I've presented this issue...and Bill needs the space for other articles! Don't worry, the full code will be uploaded to GEnie.

However, I may succumb to demands of Scroungemaster II builders, and publish the 6809 CamelForth configured for the Scroungemaster II board. Whichever I do next, I'll do the other just one installment later.

REFERENCES

1. **Derick, Mitch and Baker, Linda,** Forth Encyclopedia, Mountain View Press, Route 2 Box 429, La Honda, CA 94020 USA (1982). Word-by-word description of Fig-Forth.

2. **Ting, C. H.,** Systems Guide to fig-Forth, Offete Enterprises, 1306 South B Street, San Mateo, CA 94402 USA (1981).

3. **Ting, C. H.,** Inside F83, Offete Enterprises (1986).

4. **Ewing, Martin S.,** The Caltech Forth Manual, a Technical Report of the Owens Valley Radio Observatory (1978). This PDP-11 Forth stored a length, four characters, and a link in two 16-bit words.

5. **Sergeant, Frank,** Pygmy Forth for the IBM PC, version 1.4 (1992). Distributed by the author, available from the Forth Interest Group (P.O. Box 2154, Oakland CA 94621 USA) or on GEnie.

6. **J. E. Thomas** examined this issue thoroughly when converting Pygmy Forth to an ANSI Forth. No matter what tricks you play with relinking words, strict ANSI compliance is violated. A regrettable decision on the part of the ANS Forth team.

7. **In private communication.**

The source code for Z80 CamelForth is *now* available on GEnie as CAMEL80.ARC in the CP/M and Forth Roundtables. Really. I just uploaded it. (Apologies to those who have been waiting.)

Source code for Z80 CamelForth is available on this site at http://www.camelforth.com/public_ftp/cam80-12.zip.

FIGURE 1. Z80 CP/M CAMELFORTH MEMORY MAP

assuming CP/M BDOS starts at ED00 hex.

```
0000·+-----------------------+¶
·····|······CP/M·stuff·······|¶
0080·+-----------------------+¶
·····|·Terminal·Input·Buffer·|¶
·····|·······················|¶
0100·+-----------------------+¶
·····|·······················|¶
·····|·CamelForth·Z80·kernel·|¶
·····|·······················|¶
1700·+-----------------------+¶
·····|·User·definitions······|¶
·····|·······················|¶
·····|·······················|···/·EB00·reserved·····¶
····~~~~~~~~~~~~~~~~~~~~~~~~~··/··EB02·>IN··········¶
·····|·······················|·/···EB04·BASE·········¶
EB00·+-----------------------+/····EB06·STATE········¶
·····|·User·Area·············|·····EB08·DP···········¶
·····|·······················|\····EB0A,EB0C··'SOURCE·¶
·····|·······················|·\···EB0E·LATEST·······¶
·····|·······Parameter·Stack·|··\··EB10·HP···········¶
EC00·+-----------------------+···\·EB12·LP···········¶
·····|·······················|¶

·····|·······················|¶
·····|···HOLD·working·buffer·|¶
EC28·+-----------------------+¶
·····|·PAD·buffer············|¶
·····|·······················|¶
EC80·+-----------------------+¶
·····|·Leave·stack*··········|¶
·····|·······················|¶
·····|·······················|¶
·····|··········Return·stack·|¶
ED00·+-----------------------+¶
·····|·······················|¶
·····|··········CP/M·········|¶
·····|·······················|¶
FFFF·+-----------------------+¶
```

* used during compilation of DO..LOOPs.

FIGURE 2. HEADER STRUCTURES

```
    CamelForth        Fig-Forth

 D7            D0   D7           D0
+--------------+  +-+-+-+--------+
|              |  |1|P|S| length |
|-    link    -|  +-+-+-+--------+
|              |  |              |
+------------+-+  |-    name    -|
|      0     |P|  |              |
+-+----------+-+  ~~~~~~~~~~~~~~~~
|S|   length   |  |              |
+-+------------+  +-+           -|
|              |  |1|            |
|-    name    -|  +-+------------+
|              |  |              |
~~~~~~~~~~~~~~~~  |-    link    -|
|              |  |              |
|-            -|  +--------------+
|              |
+--------------+

   Pygmy Forth           F83

D7             D0  D7           D0
+--------------+  +--------------+
|              |  |              |
|-    view    -|  |-    view    -|
|              |  |              |
+--------------+  +--------------+
|              |  |              |
|-    link    -|  |-    lin     -|
|              |  |              |
+-+-+-+--------+  +-+-+-+--------+
|0|0|S| length |  |1|P|S| length|
+-+-+-+--------+  +-+-+-+--------+
|              |  |              |
|              |  |              |
|-    name    -|  |-    name    -|
|              |  |              |
~~~~~~~~~~~~~~~~  ~~~~~~~~~~~~~~~~
|              |  |              |
|-            -|  +-+           -|
|              |  |1|            |
+--------------+  +-+------------+
```

Link - in CamelForth and Fig-Forth, points to the previous word's Length byte. In Pygmy Forth and F83, points to the previous word's Link.

P - Precedence bit, equals 1 for an IMMEDIATE word (not used in Pygmy).

S - Smudge bit, used to prevent FIND from finding this word.

1 - in Fig-Forth and F83, the length byte and the last character of the name are flagged with a 1 in the most significant bit (bit 7).

View - in Pygmy Forth and F83, contains the block number of the source code for this word.

Continue with Part 7 | Back to publications page

MOVING FORTH by Brad Rodriguez

Part 7: CamelForth for the 8051

This article first appeared in **The Computer Journal** #71 (January/February 1995).

Under the prodding of Our Esteemed Editor, I present CamelForth for the 8051. CamelForth for the 6809 will follow soon! This 8051 Forth occupies about 6K of program memory. Alas, the full source listing would take 16 pages of TCJ, so this article includes only the significantly changed portions of the kernel. *[Note for web publication: see the end of this page for a link to the 8051 source code.]* These should illustrate how the high-level code is modified for the 8051 assembler, and for subroutine threading. The full source code is available in the Forth Roundtable on GEnie as file CAMEL51.ZIP, and the freeware 8051 assembler as file A51.ZIP. But first...

Z80 ERRATA

In the file CAMEL80H.AZM, the definition of DO is given as

```
[']  xdo ,BRANCH  . . .
```

It should be

```
[']  xdo ,XT  . . .
```

This is of no consequence on the Z80 (where ,BRANCH and ,XT are identical), but it became embarassingly obvious on the 8051.
Also, in the words S" and (S"), the word ALIGN should really be ALIGNED. On the Z80 -- and the 8051 -- both are no-ops, so this mistake didn't make itself evident.

8051 CAMELFORTH MODEL

In issue #60 I summarized the design decisions for an 8051 Forth. To recap: the 8051's retarded memory addressing practically demands the use of subroutine threading. This means the hardware stack (in the 8051 register file) is the Return Stack. The Parameter Stack (a.k.a. Data Stack) is in 256 bytes of external RAM, using R0 as the stack pointer. Since that article, I've discovered that it's better to keep the Top Of Stack item (TOS) in DPTR than in R3:R2. Thus:

reg adrs	8051 name	Forth usage
0	R0	low byte of PSP (Parameter Stack Pointer)
1-5	R1-R5	scratch registers for Forth
6-7	R6-R7	loop index
8		high byte of PSP and UP (also output on P2)
9-7Fh		119 bytes of return stack (more on 8052s!)
81h	SP	low byte of RSP (Return Stack Pointer)
82-83h	DPTR	Top-Of-Stack item
E0,F0h	A,B	scratch registers for Forth

This incorporates an idea from Charles Curley [CUR93]. On a register-rich machine like the 8051, we can keep the innermost loop index in registers. This makes LOOP and +LOOP much faster. DO must still push two values on the Return Stack: the *old* loop index, and the *new* loop limit! UNLOOP must of course restore the loop index from the Return Stack -- kudos to the ANSI team for making UNLOOP a distinct word! Note that R6:R7 are *not* the topmost Return Stack item, merely the innermost loop index.
Port 2 (P2) contains the high byte of the Parameter Stack Pointer (allowing R0 to address external memory), which is also the high byte of the User Pointer -- the low byte of UP is assumed to be 00. I learned the hard way that P2 can't be read while executing from external ROM, so I keep a copy of the P2 byte in register 8.
I have a novel implementation of BRANCH and ?BRANCH. Since the 8051 model is subroutine-threaded, high-level Forth is compiled as true machine code. So BRANCH can be implemented with an SJMP (or AJMP or LJMP) instruction. ?BRANCH can be implemented with a JZ instruction, *if* the zero/nonzero status of the top-of-stack is put in the accumulator (A register). The subroutine ZEROSENSE does this. So, BRANCH and ?BRANCH become

BRANCH:	SJMP dest	
?BRANCH:	LCALL ZEROSENSE JZ dest	

Similar routines LOOPSENSE and PLUSLOOPSENSE allow a JZ instruction to be used for LOOP and +LOOP. For these, a call to UNLOOP must appear after the JZ, to clean up the Return Stack when the program "falls out" of the loop.
In the assembly language source file I have manually replaced the sequence

```
LCALL word   RET
```

with the shorter and faster

```
LJMP word
```

in many places [CUR93]. This works as long as "word" isn't a return-stack operator (such as R> or >R). LCALL and LJMP have also been replaced with ACALL and AJMP where possible. The CamelForth compiler does *not* attempt these optimizations.

I wrote the 8051 kernel to use "Intel" byte order (low byte first). Then I discovered that the address compiled into an LJMP or LCALL is stored *high* byte first. Rather than rewrite the entire kernel, I included a byte-swap in those words which compile LCALLs: COMPILE, !CF and ,CF (all in the Dependency word set).

Listing 1 gives the 8051 assembly language "primitives", and Listing 2 gives the Dependency word set.

HARVARD ARCHITECTURES

The 8051 uses a "Harvard" architecture: program and data are kept in separate memories. In embedded systems, these are typically ROM and RAM, respectively. ANS Forth is the first Forth standard to address the restrictions of a Harvard architecture. Briefly, ANS Forth says that a) application programs can only access Data memory, and b) all of the operators used to access memory and build data structures must operate in Data space. (Ref. section 3.3.3 of the ANS document [ANS94].) This includes the Forth words

```
@ ! C@ C! DP HERE ALLOT , C, COUNT TYPE WORD (S") S" CMOVE
```

Yet the Forth compiler still needs to access Program space (also called Code or Instruction space). And Forth needs to maintain a dictionary pointer for Program space as well as Data space. So I've added these new words (shown in Listing 3):

```
I@ I! IC@ IC! IDP IHERE IALLOT I, IC, ICOUNT ITYPE IWORD (IS")
IS" D->I I->D
```

The "I" prefix stands for "Instruction" (since "P" and "C" have other meanings in Forth). ICOUNT and ITYPE are needed to display strings which have been compiled into ROM. IWORD copies the string left by WORD from Data space to Code space -- needed to build Forth word headers and ROMmed strings. D->I and I->D are equivalents of CMOVE, which copy to and from Code space.

VARIABLEs must have addresses in Data space. So they can't use the traditional practice of putting the data immediately after the Code field. Instead, the *Data space address* of the data is stored after the Code field. In essence, a VARIABLE is a CONSTANT whose value is the Data space address. (Note that the traditional CONSTANT is still valid.)

CREATEd words, and words built with CREATE...DOES>, must work the same way. Here's how they look in Program space:

CODE word:	**...header...**	**8051 machine code**
high-level:	**..header..**	**8051 machine code**
CONSTANT:	**..header..**	**LCALL-DOCON value**
VARIABLE:	**..header..**	**LCALL-DOCON Data-adrs**
CREATEd:	**..header..**	**LCALL-DOCON Data-adrs**

Note that CONSTANT must replace the value stored by CREATE, and : must "un-allot" both this value and the LCALL DOCON.

S" presents special problems. Strings defined with S" ("text literals") must reside in Data space, where they can be used by such words as TYPE and EVALUATE. But we expect those strings to be part of a definition, and to exist in ROM in a ROM forth environment. We could store the string in Program space, and copy it to HERE when referenced, but the ANS document does not allow text literals to exist in this "transient" storage region (ref. sections 3.3.3.4 and 3.3.3.6 [ANS93]). Also, if WORD returns its string at HERE -- as in CamelForth -- text literals must not alter this transient region.

My solution is to have S" *store* the string in Code space, but permanently reserve space for it in Data space, and copy it from Code to Data when referenced. ANS Forth does not yet fully address the problems of Harvard processors; something like C's "initialized data" region may eventually be required.

Since ." strings can never be accessed by the programmer, they *can* be stored in Code space, using the words (IS") and IS". (These are the "old" (S") and S".) This adds two words to the kernel, but saves quite a bit of Data space. I plan to move the string-literal words into either the Dependency word set, or a new "Harvard" word set.

WRITING TO PROGRAM SPACE

The 8051 can't actually write to Program memory. There's no hardware signal for this, and no machine instruction. Under these circumstances, the CamelForth *interpreter* will work, but new words can't be compiled. You can get around this by causing some memory to appear in *both* Program and Data space.

Figure 1 shows the modification to my board, an MCB8031 from Blue Ridge Micros (2505 Plymouth Road, Johnson City, TN, 37601, USA, telephone 615-335-6696, fax 615-929-3164). U1A and U1B create a new read strobe which is active for *either* a Program or Data fetch. EPROM is selected only when A15 is low (lower 32K), and RAM when A15 is high (upper 32K). You still can't write to EPROM, of course, but you *can* execute programs out of RAM! One disadvantage: this makes @ and I@ equivalent, so it's not immediately obvious if the wrong one was used somewhere.

Figure 1

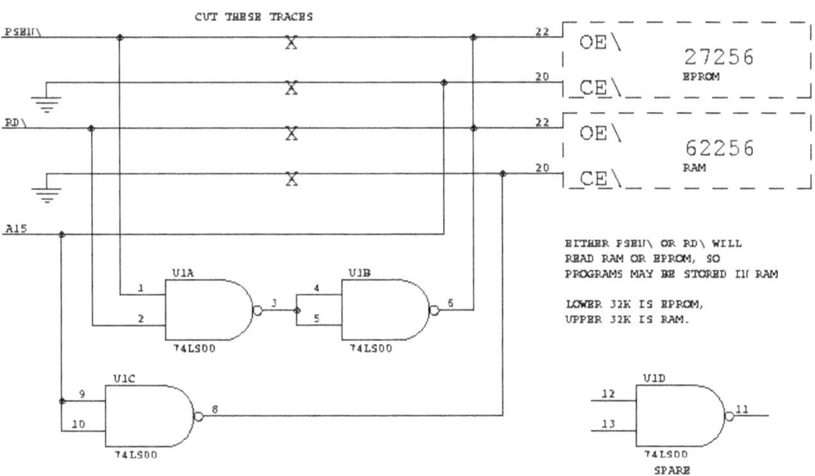

NEXT ISSUE...

These modifications to the CamelForth high-level code are intended to be portable to *either* Harvard or non-Harvard ("von Neumann") machines. For the latter, the new Program-space words are simply equated to their Data-space equivalents, e.g. on the Z80,

IFETCH	EQU	FETCH
ISTORE	EQU	STORE
ITYPE	EQU	TYPE

etc.

In the next installment I shall modify the *8051* source code to work on the 6809...thus approaching a truly portable model by successive approximation.

REFERENCES

[ANS93] dpANS-6 draft proposed American National Standard for Information Systems - Programming Languages - Forth, June 30, 1993. "It is distributed solely for the purpose of review and comment and should not be used as a design document. It is inappropriate to claim compatibility with this draft standard." Nevertheless, for the last 16 months it's all we've had to go by.

[CUR93] Curley, Charles, Optimization Considerations, Forth Dimensions XIV:5 (Jan/Feb 1993), pp. 6-12.

Source code for 8051 CamelForth is available on this site at
http://www.camelforth.com/public_ftp/cam51-15.zip.

Continue with Part 8 | Back to publications page

MOVING FORTH by Brad Rodriguez

Part 8: CamelForth for the 6809

This article first appeared in **The Computer Journal** #74 (July/August 1995).

Finally, the last installment of "Moving Forth!" Here is the long- promised ANSI CamelForth for the Motorola 6809, and specifically for the Scroungmaster II processor board.

Unlike the Z80 and 8051 CamelForth, the 6809 Forth was produced with my "Chromium 2" Forth metacompiler [ROD92]. Right away you'll notice two things: first, the metacompiler runs on an older Forth (F83), and so the source code is contained in 16x64 Forth "screens". I've converted these to an ASCII file for TCJ, but the original formatting is still evident.

Second, source code for a Forth metacompiler looks like ordinary Forth code (with a few changes, which I'll discuss shortly). Thus the definition of **1+** is given as

CODE 1+	1 # ADDD,	NEXT	;C

The assembler used is the 6809 assembler I've described previously in TCJ [ROD91].

I typed the high-level source code directly from the already-published listings (converting to the Forth syntax in the process). Unfortunately, this was done over the space of a few days, and sometimes I worked from the Z80 listing, and sometimes the 8051...with the result that the Harvard-architecture constructs (such as I@ and IALLOT) are not consistently used in the 6809 code. This is of no consequence for the non-Harvard 6809, but I'll have to correct this before porting the Forth code to a Harvard CPU.

Also, since I was working from published listings, I often neglected typing the detailed comments for the high-level words. For this I apologize. You can find how any word works by consulting the previous listings, but I shouldn't force you to do this.

6809 CAMELFORTH SOURCE CODE

The 6809 CamelForth model holds top-of-stack in D, and uses the S stack pointer for the Parameter Stack. The U stack pointer is the Return Stack Pointer, and Y is the Interpreter Pointer. X is the temporary register "W". The 6809 direct page pointer DPR holds the high byte of the User Pointer (the low byte is assumed to be zero).

The memory map for a Scroungemaster II with 8K of RAM and 8K of EPROM is as follows:

6000-797Fh	RAM dictionary (for new definitions)
7980-79FFh	Terminal Input Buffer
7A00-7A7Fh	User Area (USER variables)
7A80-7AFFh	Parameter Stack (grows downward)
7B00-7B27h	HOLD area (grows downward)
7B28-7B7Fh	PAD area (general purpose buffer)
7B80-7BFFh	Return Stack (grows downward)

E000-FFFFh	Forth kernel in EPROM

All of the RAM data areas are referenced to the User Pointer, whose starting value is given by UP-INIT: in this case, 7A00h. (Note the use of UP-INIT-HI for the high byte of this value.) When CamelForth starts, it will set its Dictionary Pointer to DP-INIT, which must be in RAM so you can add new definitions to the Forth dictionary. These are all specified with the metacompiler's EQU directive. An EQU is like a CONSTANT, except that it is *only* known to the metacompiler. These EQUates take up no space in the 6809 kernel, and will not appear in the 6809 Forth's dictionary.

DICTIONARY tells the metacompiler where to compile the code, in this case for an 8K EPROM from E000-FFFFh. The new dictionary is named "ROM", and then ROM is specified to select that dictionary. (If you're familiar with Forth vocabularies, you'll see a strong resemblance.)

AKA ("also known as") defines a synonym for a Forth word. Since the 6809 is a non-Harvard machine, we should compile @ wherever I@ appears in the source code, and likewise for the other "I-prefix" (instruction-space) words. AKA will do this. These synonyms are like EQUates -- they don't appear in the 6809 dictionary.

The metacompiler allows you to use forward references, i.e., Forth words which haven't been defined yet. (You must of course define them before you finish!) Often this is automatic, but AKA requires you to explicitly declare a forward reference with PRESUME. Thus

```
PRESUME WORD  AKA WORD IWORD
```

is needed to create the IWORD synonym. @ ! HERE ALLOT and the others are PRESUMEd by the metacompiler, so we don't have to do so here.

The CODE definitions are conventional. Note that you can use

```
HERE EQU labelname
```

to generate a label when metacompiling. (This is a function of the metacompiler, not the assembler.) Also, ASM: begins a "fragment" of assembler code (i.e., not part of a CODE word).
The phrase

```
HERE RESOLVES name
```

is used to resolve certain forward references which are made by the metacompiler (for example, the metacompiler has to know where the code for the DOCOLON action is). You should leave these alone. Otherwise, feel free to add any CODE definitions to the source code.
The code for defining words and control structures (IMMEDIATE words) is rather opaque. This is because these words *must also perform some action while metacompiling.* For example: the 6809 Forth includes the standard word CONSTANT, to define new constants. But CONSTANTs may also appear in the 6809 kernel; we may have to define a CONSTANT *while metacompiling*. The EMULATE: phrase instructs the metacompiler how to handle the word CONSTANT if it is encountered. This phrase is written entirely using metacompiler words, and so may appear to be total gibberish.
Likewise, IF THEN and their ilk include the metacompiler phrases to build and resolve branches in the 6809 image. Some Forth metacompilers bury this code inside the compiler. This makes for prettier target code, but if you change the way branches work (for example), you have to perform surgery on the metacompiler. I preferred to make these actions easily changeable, and so I designed Chromium to put them in the target source code. (The most horrific examples are the definitions of TENDLOOP and TS", which actually extend the metacompiler vocabulary in the middle of the target source code.)
If you're new to Forth and the metacompiler, it's best to just accept these as given. "Ordinary" colon definitions are easy to add. Just follow the example of the rest of the 6809 source code. You can even make CREATE..DOES> definitions, as long as you don't need to use them within the metacompiler.

FUTURE WORK

On a 1 MHz 6809, a line of text input takes a noticeable time to process (up to 1 second at a rough estimate). This is partly becuase so much of the interpreter is written in high-level Forth, and partly because CamelForth uses a single-linked-list dictionary. These handicaps only affect *compilation* speed, not execution speed, but the delays can be annoying. Maybe someday I'll do an article on "Accelerating Forth".
Currently, the User Pointer never changes. The reason we have a User Pointer is to support multitasking -- each task having separate user area, stacks, etc. I'll be

working on this soon. I may also explore using the SM II's memory management to give each task a full 32K private dictionary. And of course, I intend to write a true *multiprocessor* Forth kernel using the shared bus. If I live long enough, a *distributed* Forth kernel using the serial ports (a la Transputer) is the logical next step.

The source code for 6809 CamelForth, version 1.0, is available on GEnie's Forth Roundtable in the file CAM09-10.ZIP. This file includes the Chromium 2 metacompiler, complete and ready to run. You'll need a copy of F83. Then you merely type

F83 CHROMIUM.SCR
1 LOAD
BYE

This will load the metacompiler, compile the 6809 CamelForth, and write the result to an Intel hex file 6809.HEX. Note: if you're using the CP/M or Atari ST versions of F83, you'll have to edit the load screen to delete the hex file utility, since this only works under MS- DOS. I haven't yet tested Chromium 2 with CP/M or Atari ST, so if you need assistance, please contact me.

Which reminds me: I have a *new email address!* You can now reach me as bj@genie.com, or just BJ if you're a GEnie user. It's a lot easier to type. *[Note for web publication: my current email address is here.]*

ERRATA

There were some errors in the Harvard memory access in CamelForth/8051. The corrected file is on GEnie as CAM51-11.ZIP. I've also uploaded the current Z80 CamelForth, CAM80-12.ZIP, which incorporates all the fixes which have been published in TCJ.

REFERENCES

[ROD91] Rodriguez, B. J., "B.Y.O. Assembler," The Computer Journal #52 (Sep/Oct 1991) and #54 (Jan/Feb 1992).

[ROD92] Rodriguez, B. J., "Principles of Metacompilation," Forth Dimensions XIV:3 (Sep/Oct 1992), XIV:4 (Nov/Dec 1992), and XIV:5 (Jan/Feb 1993). Describes the "Chromium 1" metacompiler.

Source code for 6809 CamelForth is available on this site at http://www.camelforth.com/public_ftp/cam09-10.zip.

Return to publications page

A Minimal TTL Processor for Architecture Exploration

Bradford J. Rodriguez - McMaster University

Keywords: CPU, processors, architecture, education

Computer architecture is presently taught "hands-on" only when adequate VLSI design tools are available. The PISC is a processor constructed from discrete TTL logic, which illustrates the operation of both hardwired and microcoded CPUs. An efficient stack machine is easy to implement, and simple hardware modifications demonstrate interrupts, memory segmentation, microsequencers, parallelism, and pipelining. A standalone PISC board should be an economical and effective tool for teaching processor design.

Introduction

The study of computer architecture is often an abstract, paper exercise. Students cannot probe the inner workings of a single-chip microprocessor, and few discrete-logic machines are open to student inspection. Only universities that have VLSI design tools can give hands-on experience in processor design and implementation. Less fortunate institutions can only offer their students "book learning."

The Pathetic Instruction Set Computer is a model processor constructed entirely of discrete logic, illustrating the principles of both hardwired and microprogrammed CPUs. Requiring only 22 standard TTL chips (excluding memory), it is well within the ability of a student to construct and understand. Its writeable microprogram store uses inexpensive EPROM and RAM. Being fully static, it can be run at slow clock speeds or manually single-stepped for observation. Simple extensions demonstrate interrupts, split instruction and data spaces, microsequencers, parallelism, and pipelining.

The Basic Processor

The PISC-1a processor (Fig. 1) is designed to achieve a maximum of functionality with a minimum of logic. It is remarkable for having only 16 internal control signals, and thus a horizontal (unencoded) microinstruction only 16 bits long!

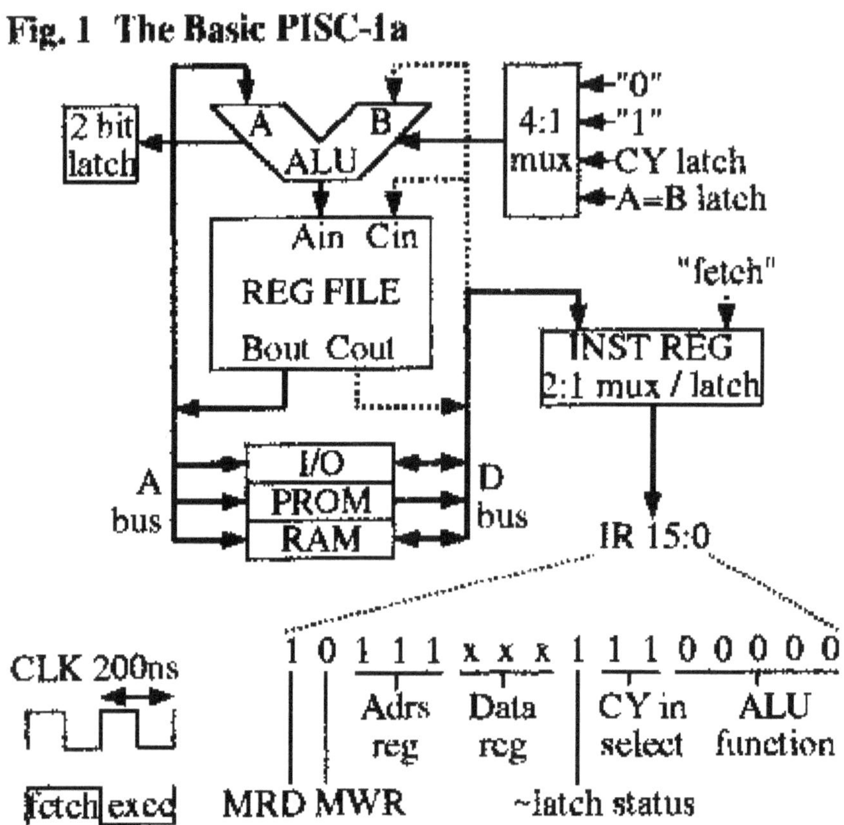

Fig. 1 The Basic PISC-1a

The ALU comprises four 74181s, which can perform the arithmetic operations of add, subtract, increment, and decrement, plus all logical operations, on 16-bit numbers. A programmable status latch and a 4-way multiplexer for the carry input complete the ALU logic. Eight 74172s provide eight 16-bit registers in a three-port register file. This file may simultaneously write one register ("A"), read a second ("B"), and read or write a third ("C"). In a single clock cycle, the following occurs:

a) one register is output to the Address bus and the ALU's A input;
b1) another register may be output to the Data bus and the ALU's B input; or
b2) data from memory may be input to another register;
c) an ALU function is applied to A (and perhaps B) and the result is stored in the first (address) register.

There is no dedicated microsequencer; its functions are performed by the ALU and register file. Every microinstruction has two phases: fetch and execute. During the fetch phase (illustrated in Fig. 1) a hardwired "pseudo-instruction" is executed:

a) output R7 (the program counter) to the Address bus and the ALU's A input;
b) read data from memory;
c) apply the function A+1 and store the result back in R7 (at the trailing edge of the clock).

Dedicated logic causes the memory data to be stored in the Instruction Register (IR) rather than in the register file. During the execute phase, this instruction is performed and the fetch instruction is reloaded into the IR. Thus every microinstruction requires two clock cycles. The control logic for this (not shown) involves only two flip-flops and a NAND gate.
Microprogram store and main program store are one and the same. Indeed, the PISC has characteristics of both a hardwired CPU and a microcoded CPU.

PISC as a Hardwired CPU

The PISC may be viewed as a conventional CPU with a hardwired control unit, a register-register architecture [3], and a badly encoded instruction set vaguely reminiscent of the PDP-11.
ALU operations are one- or two-operand, and include register-register move, add, add with carry, subtract, subtract with borrow, increment, decrement, left shift, and all logical functions. There is no multiply, divide, or right shift.
Memory operations are load and store, and have three addressing modes: register indirect, register indirect with postincrement, or register indirect with postdecrement. Postincrement addressing on R7 (the program counter) yields immediate addressing.
Control instructions are ALU operations on the program counter. Register indirect jump (absolute or relative) and conditional skip can be done in a single instruction. Other jumps and branches, and subroutine call/return, must be explicitly coded.

PISC as a Microprogrammed CPU

The PISC instruction word actuates physical control signals, and one can view the PISC as a microprogrammed CPU. The basic PISC implements a conventional machine inefficiently, since it lacks the logic to separate and decode the fields of a macroinstruction. But the PISC excels as a zero-operand architecture, i.e., a stack machine.

The fastest implementation uses threaded code [1] and a 16-bit macroinstruction. This reduces the microinterpreter to one microinstruction:

```
MRD PC,IP,A+1 ; mem(IP)->PC, IP+1->IP
```

One register is dedicated as the macro Instruction Pointer, and one or two others as stack pointers. Some flexibility can be gained by adding one microinstruction to the interpreter to use indirect threaded code [2].

Logically, the microprogram store should be separate from the macroprogram memory. But a unified macro- and micro-program store allows the programmer to write microcode and add new macroinstructions -- a valuable educational tool. Such an "extensible instruction set" in a stack machine is evocative of the programming language Forth, and this concept has been anticipated by several dedicated Forth processors [4].

Glaring Deficiencies

Many weaknesses of the PISC become evident after a short period of use, including:

a) no conditional branch microinstruction -- an important need [6];
b) no provision for literal values in the microinstruction;
c) no ALU logic for multiply, divide, and right shift;
d) no logic for decoding of macroinstructions;
e) no provision for interrupts;
f) sparse coding of the ALU function select; and
g) two clocks required per microinstruction.

It can be argued that the PISC is a valuable educational tool because these faults, and several potential solutions, are painfully obvious. Some faults cannot be rectified without substantial added logic, or an expansion of the microinstruction word. But several improvements are trivial.

ALU Operation Decoding

Seven bits of the 16-bit microinstruction (including the carry input select) select the ALU function. Fewer than 32 of the 128 codes are actually useful, however. A "nanocode" memory [3], or combinational logic, could reduce the ALU field(s) from seven to five bits.

Alternatively, unused function codes can be decoded to generate auxiliary control signals. For example, the carry input select (IR6:5) is a "don't-care" for logic operations (IR4=1). Thus 48 of the 64 logic function codes can be used for other purposes. A single 74138 can provide eight supplementary control signals, such as interrupt enable and disable. Additional logic can prevent the ALU output from being written to a register, if desired.

Conditional ALU Operations

A simple conditional microinstruction modifies the ALU function according to the carry status. Two modifications are useful:

a) if carry set, change ALU operation from "A" to "B" (conditional jump)

b) if carry set, change ALU operation from "A" to "A+B" (conditional branch)

Unused ALU functions can be decoded for these operations, and suitable logic added to alter the ALU function select inputs. This does, however, add delay to the critical timing path of the CPU.

Interrupts

Two kinds of interrupts can be added easily to the PISC. Microinterrupts can be implemented by having the interrupt set a flip-flop, changing the program counter in the fetch pseudo- instruction from R7 to R6. R6 must be dedicated as an interrupt service register, and an additional control signal must be decoded to reset the flip-flop. (The RCA 1802 used a similar interrupt scheme.)

Macrointerrupts can be recognized by the microinterpreter by adding a conditional skip and an interrupt service routine to the microinterpreter. The interrupt input is connected to the carry input multiplexer, replacing the little-used A=B input. The interpreter is slowed by only one microinstruction.

In either case, registers and the status latch must be saved and restored by microcode. Logic to disable the interrupt inputs is desirable.

Multiple Memory Spaces

Many processors, such as the PDP-11, enforce a division of instruction and data space. Since the bits that select the PISC address register are available, and R7 is the program counter, a three-input NAND gate can produce an "instruction space" enable signal. This signal is correctly asserted for immediate addressing mode.

Further segmentation of the memory space depends upon the register assignment for the macro machine. One 2-to-4 decoder can identify microcode, macrocode, stack, and data spaces in the threaded stack machine. (This is suggestive of the 80x86.)

Parallelism

If the microcode memory space is separate from main memory, the fetch and execute phases can occur in parallel, and each microinstruction can execute in one clock cycle (Fig. 2). A 12-bit (optionally 16-bit) counter serves as a rudimentary microsequencer. This liberates the ALU from its sequencer role, and eliminates the need for the fetch pseudo-instruction. Each clock cycle fetches a microinstruction from the microprogram ROM.

Fig. 2 Parallel Fetch and Execute

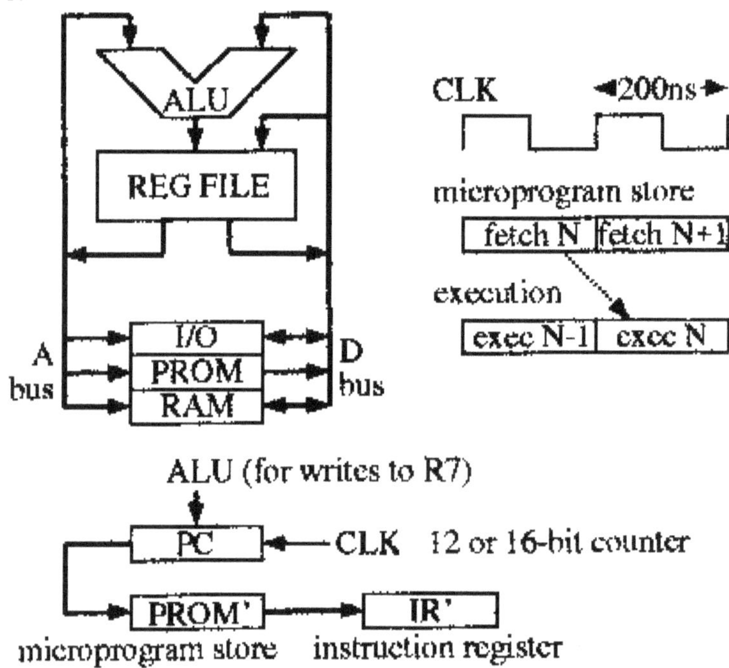

Absolute jumps are still possible by loading the counter from the ALU or Data bus. But ALU operations on the program counter are no longer permitted, eliminating the relative branch, conditional skip, and immediate addressing capabilities. Microinterrupts are also lost; macrointerrupts become impractical.

Since each microinstruction is executed one clock cycle after it is fetched (Fig. 2), a jump instruction will experience a one-clock-cycle delay, and the instruction following a jump will always be executed. This is the "delayed branch" seen in most microprogrammed machines and some pipelined RISC machines.

With this configuration, a main memory access need not complete in one clock cycle. The limiting factors in clock speed are the ALU path and the microinstruction ROM. Preliminary studies indicate that the clock speed of the PISC can be doubled, with two clock cycles required for a main memory reference.

Load/Store (RISC-like) Operation

A further modification (Fig. 3) re-unifies the microcode and macrocode memories. During ALU operations the address buffer is disabled, and fetch and execution remain simultaneous. But during a memory load or store, the output of the PC is tri-stated and the address buffer enabled, allowing the ALU to address the main memory (PROM' and RAM'). The count input of the PC is also disabled, and the IR is loaded with a "dummy" instruction (NOP). After the memory access is complete, the dummy instruction executes and the PC fetches the next instruction.

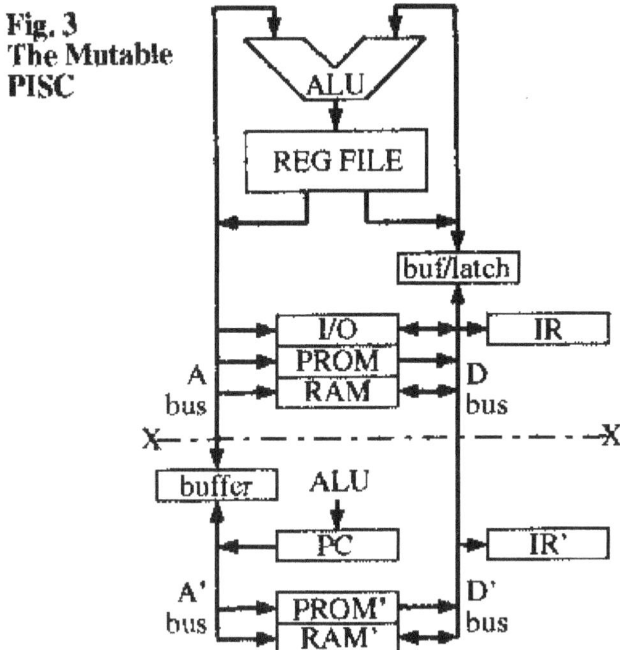

Fig. 3 The Mutable PISC

In this configuration the PISC can be viewed as a load/store architecture [3]. Like a RISC machine, all instructions execute in one clock cycle, except for memory references which require two.

If the address buffer is bidirectional, the PC can be routed to the ALU. This restores the relative branch, conditional skip, and immediate addressing capabilities.

The "Mutable PISC"

It would be unreasonable to hand students "a bag of parts" and a wirewrap tool, and expect them to construct the PISC as a class exercise. More attractive to the student, and perhaps less attractive to the experimenter, would be a printed-circuit-board of the basic PISC and its simpler enhancements. This is envisioned as the PISC-2 (Fig. 3).

The PISC-2 will use the Am29705 register file instead of the obsolescent and scarce 74172. This will require the addition of a 16-bit Data latch, and a few more control signals. Rather than expand the microinstruction word, a minimal function decoder will be added.

By judicious insertion and removal of components, the PISC-2 can be configured as a PISC-1 (two-clock instructions), a separate microprogram machine, or a load/store machine. Program development in the "unified memory" configurations could be via keypad and display, or an RS-232 serial port, using an on-board monitor program.

Conclusions

An educational drawback of the PISC is its abysmal implementation of "conventional" (1- or 2-operand) macromachines. This is a consequence of the PISC's original "mission": a stack processor using a minimum of standard TTL logic (2100 gates). But the PISC-1 vividly teaches that power does not necessarily imply complexity. Compare the speed of a 5 MHz PISC-1a to a 5 MHz 8086, when executing eForth primitives (given as number of 200 nsec clock cycles):

Primitive	PISC	8086
NEXT	4	23
EXECUTE	4	19
DROP	6	29
EXIT	6	39
BRANCH	8	36
DUP	8	46
@	10	52
LIT	10	46

R>	10	50
R@	10	44
>R	10	51
!	10	53
ENTER	10	49
OVER	12	50
AND	12	53
0<	14	47
SWAP	12	61
?BRANCH	16	51/56
UM+	18	69

A processor design remarkably similar to the PISC, the QS2, has been successfully used in a VLSI design course [5]. The PISC has the advantage of being built from standard TTL; thus, it is within the reach of even the most impoverished institutions and students.

References

1. Bell, James R., "Threaded Code," Communications of the ACM, Vol. 16 No. 6 (June 1973), pp. 370-372.
2. Dewar, Robert B. K., "Indirect Threaded Code," Communications of the ACM, Vol. 18 No. 6 (June 1975), pp. 330-331.
3. Hennessy, John L. and Patterson, David A., Computer Architecture: A Quantitative Approach, Morgan Kaufmann Publishers, San Mateo, CA (1990).
4. Koopman, Philip J., Stack Computers: the new wave, Ellis Horwood Ltd., Chichester, England (1989).
5. Rible, John, "QS2: RISCing it all," Proceedings of the 1991 FORML Conference, Forth Interest Group, Oakland, CA (1991), pp. 156-159.
6. Stallings, William, Computer Organization and Architecture, Macmillan Publishing Co., New York (1987).

Schematic Diagram

The schematic diagram of the PISC-1a is available if you have Adobe Acrobat or another .PDF reader. **Thanks to Derry Bryson** for converting the schematics to PDF files.

B.Y.O. ASSEMBLER

-or-

Build Your Own (Cross-) Assembler.in Forth

by Brad Rodriguez

http://www.bradrodriguez.com/papers/tcjassem.txt

A. INTRODUCTION

In a previous issue of this journal I described how to "bootstrap" yourself into a new processor, with a simple debug monitor. But how do you write code for this new CPU, when you can't find or can't afford an assembler? Build your own!

Forth is an ideal language for this. I've written cross-assemblers in as little as two hours (for the TMS320, over a long lunch break). Two days is perhaps more common; and one processor (the Zilog Super8) took me five days. But when you have more time than money, this is a bargain.

In part 1 of this article I will describe the basic principles of Forth-style assemblers -- structured, single-pass, postfix. Much of this will apply to any processor, and these concepts are in almost every Forth assembler.

In part 2 I will examine an assembler for a specific CPU: the Motorola 6809. This assembler is simple but not trivial, occupying 15 screens of source code. Among other things, it shows how to handle instructions with multiple modes (in this case, addressing modes). By studying this example, you can figure out how to handle the peculiarities of your own CPU.

B. WHY USE FORTH?

I believe that Forth is the easiest language in which to write assemblers.

First and foremost, Forth has a "text interpreter" designed to look up text strings and perform some related action.
Turning text strings into bytes is exactly what is needed to compile assembler mnemonics! Operands and addressing modes can also be handled as Forth "words."

Forth also includes "defining words," which create large sets of words with a common action. This feature is very useful when defining assembler mnemonics.

Since every Forth word is always available, Forth's arithmetic and logical functions can be used within the assembler environment to perform address and operand arithmetic.

Finally, since the assembler is entirely implemented in Forth words, Forth's "colon definitions" provide a rudimentary macro facility, with no extra effort.

C. THE SIMPLEST CASE: ASSEMBLING A NOP

To understand how Forth translates mnemonics to machine code, consider the simplest case: the NOP instruction (12 hex on the 6809).

A conventional assembler, on encountering a NOP in the opcode field, must append a 12H byte to the output file and advance the location counter by 1. Operands and comments are ignored. (I will ignore labels for the time being.)

In Forth, the memory-resident dictionary is usually the output "file." So, make NOP a Forth word, and give it an action, namely, "append 12H to the dictionary and advance the dictionary pointer."

```
HEX
: NOP, 12 C, ;
```

Assembler opcodes are often given Forth names which include a trailing comma, as shown above. This is because many Forth words -- such as AND XOR and OR -- conflict with assembler mnemonics. The simplest solution is to change the assembler mnemonics slightly, usually with a trailing comma. (This comma is a Forth convention, indicating that something is appended to the dictionary.)

D. THE CLASS OF "INHERENT" OPCODES

Most processors have many instructions, like NOP, which require no operands. All of these could be defined as Forth colon definitions, but this duplicates code, and wastes a lot of space. It's much more efficient to use Forth's "defining word" mechanism to give all of these words a common action. In object-oriented parlance, this builds "instances" of a single "class."

This is done with Forth's CREATE and DOES>. (In fig-Forth, as used in the 6809 assembler, the words are <BUILDS and DOES>.)

: INHERENT	(Defines the name of the class)
CREATE	(this will create an instance)
C,	(store the parameter for each instance)
DOES>	(this is the class' common action)
C@	(get each instance's parameter)
C,	(the assembly action, as above)
;	(End of definition)

HEX	
12 INHERENT NOP,	(Defines an instance NOP,
	of class INHERENT, with
	parameter 12H.)
3A INHERENT ABX,	(Another instance
	- the ABX instr)
3D INHERENT MUL,	(Another instance
	- the MUL instr)

In this case, the parameter (which is specific to each instance) is simply the opcode to be assembled for each instruction.

This technique provides a substantial memory savings, with almost no speed penalty. But the real advantage becomes evident when complex instruction actions -- such as required for parameters, or addressing modes -- are involved.

E. HANDLING OPERANDS

Most assembler opcodes, it is true, require one or more operands. As part of the action for these instructions, Forth routines could be written to parse text from the input stream, and interpret this text as operand fields. But why? The Forth envrionment already provides a parse-and-interpret mechanism!

So, Forth will be used to parse operands. Numbers are parsed normally (in any base!), and equates can be Forth CONSTANTs. But, since the operands determine how the opcode is handled, they will be processed first. The results of operand parsing will be left on Forth's stack, to be picked up by the opcode word. This leads to Forth's unique postfix format for assemblers: operands, followed by opcode.

Take, for example, the 6809's ORCC instruction, which takes a single numeric parameter:

HEX
: ORCC, 1A C, C, ;

The exact sequence of actions for ORCC, is: 1) put 1A hex on the parameter stack; 2) append the top stack item (the 1A) to the dictionary, and drop it from the stack; 3) append the new top stack item (the operand) to the dictionary, and drop it from the stack. It is assumed that a numeric value was already on the stack, for the second C, to use. This numeric value is the result of the operand parsing, which, in this case, is simply the parsing of a single integer value:

HEX
0F ORCC,

The advantage here is that all of Forth's power to operate on stack values, via both built-in operators and newly-defined functions, can be employed to create and modify operands.
For example:

HEX	
01 CONSTANT CY-FLAG	(a "named" numeric value)
02 CONSTANT OV-FLAG	
04 CONSTANT Z-FLAG	
CY-FLAG Z-FLAG + ORCC,	(add 1 and 4
	to get operand)

The extension of operand-passing to the defining words technique is straightforward.

F. HANDLING ADDRESSING MODES

Rarely can an operand, or an opcode, be used unmodified. Most of the instructions in a modern processor can take multiple forms, depending on the programmer's choice of addressing mode.

Forth assemblers have attacked this problem in a number of ways, depending on the requirements of the specific processor. All of these techniques remain true to the Forth methodology: the addressing mode operators are implemented as Forth words. When these words are executed, they alter the assembly of the current instruction.

1. **Leaving additional parameters on the stack.**
   This is most useful when an addressing mode must Always be specified. The addressing-mode word leaves some constant value on the stack, to be picked up by the opcode word. Sometimes this value can be a "magic number" which can be added to the opcode to modify it for the different mode. When this is not feasible, the addressing-mode value can activate a CASE statement within the opcode, to select one of several actions. In this latter case, instructions of different lengths, possibly with different operands, can be assembled depending on the addressing mode.

2. **Setting flags or values in fixed variables.**
   This is most useful when the addressing mode is optional. Without knowing whether an addressing mode was specified, you don't know if the value on the stack is a "magic number" or just an operand value. The solution: have the addressing mode put its magic number in a predefined variable (often called MODE). This variable is initialized to a default value, and reset to this default value after each instruction is assembled. Thus, this variable can be tested to see if an addressing mode was specified (overriding the default).

3. **Modifying parameter values already on the stack.**
   It is occasionally possible to implement addressing mode words that work by modifying an operand value. This is rarely seen.

All three of these techniques are used, to some extent, within the 6809 assembler.

For most processors, register names can simply be Forth CONSTANTs, which leave a value on the stack. For some processors, it is useful to have register names specify "register addressing mode" as well. This is easily done by defining register names with a new defining word, whose run-time action sets the addressing mode (either on the stack or in a MODE variable).

Some processors allow multiple addressing modes in a single instruction. If the number of addressing modes is fixed by the instruction, they can be left on the stack. If the number of addressing modes is variable, and it is desired to know how many have been specified, multiple MODE variables can be used for the first, second, etc. (In one case – the Super8 -- I had to keep track of not only how many addressing modes were specified, but also where among the operands they were specified. I did this by saving the stack position along with each addressing mode.)

Consider the 6809 ADD instruction. To simplify things, ignore the Indexed addressing modes for now, and just consider the remaining three addressing modes: Immediate, Direct, and Extended. These will be specified as follows:

	source code	**assembles as**
Immediate:	**number # ADD,**	**8B nn**
Direct:	**address <> ADD,**	**9B aa**
Extended:	**address ADD,**	**BB aa aa**

Since Extended has no addressing mode operator, the mode-variable approach seems to be indicated. The Forth words # and <> will set MODE.

Observe the regularity in the 6809 opcodes. If the Immediate opcode is the "base" value, then the Direct opcode is this value plus 10 hex, and the Extended opcode is this value plus 30 hex. (And the Indexed opcode, incidentally, is this value plus 20 hex.) This applies uniformly across almost all 6809 instructions which use these addressing modes. (The exceptions are those opcodes whose Direct opcodes are of the form 0x hex.)

Regularities like this are made to be exploited! This is a general rule for writing assemblers: find or make an opcode chart, and look for regularities -- especially those applying to addressing modes or other instruction modifiers (like condition codes).

In this case, appropriate MODE values are suggested:

VARIABLE MODE HEX
: # 0 MODE ! ;
: <> 10 MODE ! ;
: RESET 30 MODE ! ;

The default MODE value is 30 hex (for Extended mode), so a Forth word RESET is added to restore this value. RESET will be used after every instruction is assembled.

The ADD, routine can now be written. Let's go ahead and write it using a defining word:

HEX	
: GENERAL-OP	\ base-opcode --
CREATE C,	
DOES>	\ operand --
C@	\ get the base opcode
MODE @ +	\ add the "magic number"
C,	\ assemble the opcode
MODE @ CASE	
0 OF C, ENDOF	\ byte operand
10 OF C, ENDOF	\ byte operand
30 OF , ENDOF	\ word operand
ENDCASE	
RESET ;	
8B GENERAL-OP ADD,	

Each "instance" of GENERAL-OP will have a different base opcode. When ADD, executes, it will fetch this base opcode, add the MODE value to it, and assemble that byte. Then it will take the operand which was passed on the stack, and assemble it either as a byte or word operand, depending on the selected mode. Finally, it will reset MODE.

Note that all of the code is now defined to create instructions in the same family as ADD:

HEX 89 GENERAL-OP ADC,
84 GENERAL-OP AND,
85 GENERAL-OP BIT,
etc.

The memory savings from defining words really become evident now. Each new opcode word executes the lengthy bit of DOES> code given above; but each word is only a one-byte Forth definition (plus header and code field, of course).

This is not the actual code from the 6809 assembler – there are additional special cases which need to be handled. But it demonstrates that, by storing enough mode information, and by making liberal use of CASE statements, the most ludicrous instruction sets can be assembled.

G. HANDLING CONTROL STRUCTURES

The virtues of structured programming, have long been sung -- and there are countless "structured assembly" macro packages for conventional assemblers. But Forth assemblers favor label-free, structured assembly code for a pragmatic reason: in Forth, it's simpler to create assembler structures than labels!

The structures commonly included in Forth assemblers are intended to resemble the programming structures of high-level Forth. (Again, the assembler structures are usually distinguished by a trailing comma.)

1. BEGIN, ... UNTIL,

The BEGIN, ... UNTIL, construct is the simplest assembler structure to understand. The assembler code is to loop back to the BEGIN point, until some condition is satisfied. The Forth assembler syntax is

```
BEGIN,    more code    cc UNTIL,
```

where 'cc' is a condition code, which has presumably been defined -- either as an operand or an addressing mode – for the jump instructions.

Obviously, the UNTIL, will assemble a conditional jump. The sense of the jump must be "inverted" so that if 'cc' is satisfied, the jump does NOT take place, but instead the code "falls through" the jump. The conventional assembler equivalent would be:

xxx:	
	...
	...
	JR ~cc,xxx

(where ~cc is the logical inverse of cc.)

Forth offers two aids to implementing BEGIN, and UNTIL,. The word HERE will return the current location counter value. And values may be kept deep in the stack, with no effect on Forth processing, then "elevated" when required.

So: BEGIN, will "remember" a location counter, by placing its value on the stack. UNTIL, will assemble a conditional jump to the "remembered" location.

: BEGIN,	(- a)	HERE ;
: UNTIL,	(a cc -)	NOTCC JR, ;

This introduces the common Forth stack notation, to indicate that BEGIN, leaves one value (an address) on the stack. UNTIL, consumes two values (an address and a condition code) from the stack, with the condition code on top. It is presumed that a word NOTCC has been defined, which will convert a condition code to its logical inverse. It is also presumed that the opcode word JR, has been defined, which will expect an address and a condition code as operands. (JR, is a more general example than the branch instructions used in the 6809 assembler.)

The use of the stack for storage of the loop address allows
BEGIN, ... UNTIL,
constructs to be nested, as:

BEGIN, ... BEGIN, ... cc UNTIL, ... cc UNTIL,

The "inner" UNTIL, resolves the "inner" BEGIN, forming a loop wholly contained within the outer
BEGIN, ... UNTIL,
loop.

2. BEGIN, ... AGAIN,

Forth commonly provides an "infinite loop" construct, BEGIN ... AGAIN , which never exits. For the sake of completeness, this is usually implemented in the assembler as well.

Obviously, this is implemented in the same manner as BEGIN, ... UNTIL,
except that the jump which is assembled by AGAIN,

is an unconditional jump.

3. DO, ... LOOP,

Many processors offer some kind of looping instruction. Since the 6809 does not, let's consider the Zilog Super8; its Decrement-and-Jump-Non-Zero (DJNZ) instruction can use any of 16 registers as the loop counter. This can be written in structured assembler:

DO, more code r LOOP,

where r is the register used as the loop counter. Once again, the intent is to make the assembler construct resemble the high-level Forth construct.

: DO,	(- a)	HERE ;
: LOOP,	(a r -)	DJNZ, ;

Some Forth assemblers go so far as to make DO, assemble a load-immediate instruction for the loop counter -- but this loses flexibility. Sometimes the loop count isn't a constant. So I prefer the above definition of DO, .

4. IF, ... THEN,

The IF, ... THEN, construct is the simplest forward-referencing construct. If a condition is satisfied, the code within the IF,...THEN, is to be executed; otherwise, control is transferred to the first instruction after THEN,.

(Note that Forth normally employs THEN, where other languages use "endif." You can have both in your assembler.)

The Forth syntax is

cc IF, ... THEN,

for which the "conventional" equivalent is

	JP ~cc,xxx	
	...	

	...	
	...	
xxx:		

Note that, once again, the condition code must be inverted to produce the expected logical sense for IF, .

In a single pass assembler, the requisite forward jump cannot be directly assembled, since the destination address of the jump is not known when IF, is encountered. This problem is solved by causing IF, to assemble a "dummy" jump, and stack the address of the jump's operand field. Later, the word THEN, (which will provide the destination address) can remove this stacked address and "patch" the jump instruction accordingly.

: IF, (cc - a) NOT 0 SWAP JP,	**(conditional jump)**
HERE 2 - ;	**(with 2-byte operand)**

: THEN, (a) HERE SWAP ! ;	**(store HERE at the)**
	(stacked address)

IF, inverts the condition code, assembles a conditional jump to address zero, and then puts on the stack the address of the jump address field. (After JP, is assembled, the location counter HERE points past the jump instruction, so we need to subtract two to get the location of the address field.) THEN, will patch the current location into the operand field of that jump.

If relative jumps are used, additional code must be added to THEN, to calculate the relative offset.

5. IF, ... ELSE, ... THEN,

A refinement of the IF,...THEN, construct allows code to be executed if the condition is NOT satisfied. The Forth syntax is

cc IF, ... ELSE, ... THEN,

ELSE, has the expected meaning: if the first part of this statement is not executed, then the second part is.

The assembler code necessary to create this construct is:

JP	~cc,xxx	
	...	(the "if" code)
	...	
JP	yyy	
xxx:	...	(the "else" code)
	...	
yyy:		

ELSE, must modify the actions of IF, and THEN, as follows:
a) the forward jump from IF, must be patched to the start of the "else" code ("xxx"); and b) the address supplied by THEN, must be patched into the unconditional jump instruction at the end of the "if" code ("JP yyy"). ELSE, must also assemble the unconditional jump. This is done thus:

: ELSE (a - a) 0 T JP,	(unconditional jump)
HERE 2 -	(stack its address)
	(for THEN, to patch)
SWAP	(get the patch address)
	(of the IF, jump
HERE SWAP !	(patch it to the current)
	(location, i.e., the)
;	(next instruction)

Note that the jump condition 'T' assembles a "jump always" instruction. The code from IF, and THEN, can be "re-used" if the condition 'F' is defined as the condition-code inverse of 'T':

: ELSE (a - a) F IF, SWAP THEN, ;

The SWAP of the stacked addresses reverses the patch order, o that the THEN, inside ELSE, patches the original IF; and the final THEN, patches the IF, inside ELSE,. Graphically, this becomes:

IF,(1) ...	IF,(2)	THEN,(1) ...	THEN,(2)
	_______________________/		
	inside ELSE,		

IF,...THEN, and IF,...ELSE,...THEN, structures can be nested.

This freedom of nesting also extends to mixtures of these and BEGIN,...UNTIL, structures.

6. BEGIN, ... WHILE, ... REPEAT,

The final, and most complex, assembler control structure is the "while" loop in which the condition is tested at the beginning of the loop, rather than at the end.

In Forth the accepted syntax for this structure is

BEGIN, evaluate cc WHILE, loop code REPEAT,

In practice, any code -- not just condition evaluations -- may be inserted between BEGIN, and WHILE,.

What needs to be assembled is this: WHILE, will assemble a conditional jump, on the inverse of cc, to the code following the REPEAT,. (If the condition code cc is satisfied, we should "fall through" WHILE, to execute the loop code.) REPEAT, will assemble an unconditional jump back to BEGIN. Or, in terms of existing constructs:

BEGIN,(1) ... cc IF,(2) ... AGAIN,(1) THEN,(2)

Once again, this can be implemented with existing words, by means of a stack manipulation inside WHILE, to re-arrange what jumps are patched by whom:

: WHILE,	**(a cc - a a)**	**IF, SWAP ;**
: REPEAT,	**(a a -)**	**AGAIN, THEN, ;**

Again, nesting is freely permitted.

H. THE FORTH DEFINITION HEADER

In most applications, machine code created by a Forth assembler will be put in a CODE word in the Forth dictionary. This requires giving it an identifying text "name," and linking it into the dictionary list.

The Forth word CREATE performs these functions for the programmer. CREATE will parse a word from the input stream, build a new entry in the dictionary with that name, and adjust the dictionary pointer to the start of the "definition field" for this word.

Standard Forth uses the word CODE to distinguish the start of an assembler definition in the Forth dictionary. In addition to performing CREATE, the word CODE may set the assembler environment (vocabulary), and may reset variables (such as MODE) in the assembler. Some Forths may also require a "code address" field; this is set by CREATE in some systems, while others expect CODE to do this.

I. SPECIAL CASES

1. Resident vs. cross-compilation

Up to now, it has been assumed that the machine code is to be assembled into the dictionary of the machine running the assembler.

For cross-assembly and cross-compilation, code is usually assembled for the "target" machine into a different area of memory. This area may or may not have its own dictionary structure, but it is separate from the "host" machine's dictionary.

The most common and straightforward solution is to provide the host machine with a set of Forth operators to access the "target" memory space. These are made deliberately analogous to the normal Forth memory and dictionary operators, and are usually distinguished by the prefix "T".
The basic set of operators required is:

TDP	**target dictionary pointer DP**
THERE	**analogous to HERE, returns TDP**
TC,	**target byte append C,**
TC@	**target byte fetch C@**
TC!	**target byte store C!**
T@	**target word fetch @**
T!	**target word store !**

Sometimes, instead of using the "T" prefix, these words will be given identical names but in a different Forth vocabulary. (The vocabulary structure in Forth allows unambiguous use of the same word name in multiple contexts.) The 6809 assembler in Part 2 assumes this.

2. Compiling to disk

Assembler output can be directed to disk, rather than to memory. This, too, can be handled by defining a new set of dictionary, fetch, and store operators. They can be distinguished with a different prefix (such as "T" again), or put in a distinct vocabulary.

Note that the "patching" manipulations used in the single-pass control structures require a randomly-accessible output medium. This is not a problem with disk, although heavy use of control structures may result in some inefficient disk access.

3. Compiler Security

Some Forth implementations include a feature known as "compiler security," which attempts to catch mismatches of control structures. For example, the structure

```
IF, ... cc UNTIL,
```

would leave the stack balanced (UNTIL, consumes the address left by IF,), but would result in nonsense code.

The usual method for checking the match of control structures is to require the "leading" control word to leave a code value on the stack, and the "trailing" word to check the stack for the correct value. For example:

IF,	**leaves a 1;**
THEN,	**checks for a 1;**
ELSE,	**checks for a 1 and leaves a 1;**
BEGIN,	**leaves a 2;**
UNTIL,	**checks for a 2;**
AGAIN,	**checks for a 2;**
WHILE,	**checks for a 2 and leaves a 3;**
REPEAT,	**checks for a 3.**

This will detect most mismatches. Additional checks may be included for the stack imbalance caused by "unmatched" control words. (The 6809 assembler uses both of these error checks.)

The cost of compiler security is the increased complexity of the stack manipulations in such words as ELSE, and WHILE,.

Also, the programmer may wish to alter the order in which control structures are resolved, by manually re-arranging the stack; compiler security makes this more difficult.

4. Labels

Even in the era of structured programming, some programmers will insist on labels in their assembler code.

The principal problem with named labels in a Forth assembler definition is that the labels themselves are Forth words.
They are compiled into the dictionary -- usually at an inconvenient point, such as inside the machine code.
For example:

CODE	**TEST ...**	**machine code ...**
	HERE CONSTANT LABEL1	
	...	**machine code ...**
LABEL1	**NZ JP,**	

will cause the dictionary header for LABEL1 -- text, links, and all -- to be inserted in the middle of CODE. Several solutions have been proposed:

a) define labels only "outside" machine code.
Occasionally useful, but very restricted.

b) use some predefined storage locations (variables) to
provide "temporary," or local, labels.

c) use a separate dictionary space for the labels, e.g.,
as provided by the TRANSIENT scheme [3].

d) use a separate dictionary space for the machine code.
This is common practice for meta-compilation; most Forth meta- compilers support labels with little difficulty.

5. Table Driven Assemblers

Most Forth assemblers can handle the profusion of addressing modes and instruction opcodes by CASE statements and other flow-of-control constructs. These may be referred to as "procedural" assemblers.

Some processors, notably the Motorola 68000, have instruction and addressing sets so complex as to render the decision trees immense. In such cases, a more "table-driven" approach may save substantial memory and processor time.

(I avoid such processors. Table driven assemblers are much more complex to write.)

6. Prefix Assemblers

Sometimes a prefix assembler is unavoidable. (One example:
I recently translated many K of Super8 assembler code from the Zilog assembler to a Forth assembler.) There is a programming "trick" which simulates a prefix assembler, while using the assembler techniques described in this article.

Basically, this trick is to "postpone" execution of the opcode word, until after the operands have been evaluated.
How can the assembler determine when the operands are finished? Easy: when the next opcode word is encountered.

So, every opcode word is modified to a) save its own execution address somewhere, and b) execute the "saved" action of the previous opcode word. For example:

```
... JP operand   ADD operands ...
```

JP stores its execution address (and the address of its "instance" parameters) in a variable somewhere. Then, the operands are evaluated. ADD will fetch the

information saved by JP, and execute the run-time action of JP. The JP action will pick up whatever the operands left on the stack.
When the JP action returns, ADD will save its own execution address and instance parameters, and the process continues.
(Of course, JP would have executed its previous opcode.)

This is confusing. Special care must be taken for the first and last opcodes in the assembler code. If mode variables are used, the problem of properly saving and restoring them becomes nightmarish. I leave this subject as an exercise for the advanced student...or for an article of its own.

J. CONCLUSION

I've touched upon the common techniques used in Forth assemblers. Since I believe the second-best way to learn is by example, in part 2 I will present the full code for the 6809 assembler. Studying a working assembler may give you hints on writing an assembler of your own.

The BEST way to learn is by doing!

K. REFERENCES

1. **Curley, Charles, Advancing Forth.**
Unpublished manuscript (1985).

2. **Wasson, Philip, "Transient Definitions,"**
Forth Dimensions III/6 (Mar-Apr 1982), p.171.

L. ADDITIONAL SOURCES

1. **Cassady, John J., "8080 Assembler,"** Forth Dimensions III/6 (Mar-Apr 1982), pp. 180-181.
Noteworthy in that the entire assembler fits in less than 48 lines of code.

2. **Ragsdale, William F., "A FORTH Assembler for the 6502,"**
Dr. Dobb's Journal #59 (September 1981),
pp. 12-24. A simple illustration of addressing modes.

3. **Duncan, Ray, "FORTH 8086 Assembler,"**
Dr. Dobb's Journal #64
(February 1982), pp. 14-18 and 33-46.

4. **Perry, Michael A., "A 68000 Forth Assembler,"**
Dr. Dobb's Journal #83 (September 1983), pp. 28-42.

5. **Assemblers for the 8080, 8051, 6502, 68HC11, 8086,**
80386, 68000, SC32, and Transputer can be downloaded
from the Forth Interest Group (FORTH) conference
on GEnie.

B.Y.O. ASSEMBLER by Brad Rodriguez

-or-

Build Your Own (Cross-) Assembler.in Forth

B.Y.O. - Part 2: A 6809 Forth Assembler

A. INTRODUCTION

Part 1 of this two-part series described the fundamental concepts used when writing postfix, structured assemblers in Forth.

This article examines, in detail, an actual assembler for the Motorola 6809 microprocessor.

I will begin with the "programmer's guide" for the 6809 assembler.
I've found, when building assemblers, that it's helpful to write this first. This is good practice, and is also in keeping with Rodriguez' First Rule for Metacompiler Writers:

always keep in mind
what you want the result to look like!

In the off-chance that someone actually wishes to use this assembler on a 6809 project, I've also included a conversion chart from Motorola to Forth notation.
If you're ever writing an assembler for others to use, please do them a favor and make one of these charts!

Finally, I'll go over the source code, and (hopefully) explain all of the obscure tricks and techniques.

The complete source code for the 6809 assembler accompanies this article.
It is written for a fig-Forth derivative, and so will require translation for 79- or 83-Standard machines.

This code was originally a Forth screen file; it has been translated to a text file for the editor's convenience.

B. PROGRAMMER'S GUIDE

The syntax of 6809 assembler instructions are:

operand addressing-mode opcode

For many instructions the addressing mode is optional. Some instructions (TFR and EXG) have two operands.

Valid non-indexed addressing modes are:

nn #	**immediate value**
nn <>	**direct (DP-page) addressing**
nnnn	**extended addressing**
nnnn []	**extended indirect addressing**

Valid indexed addressing modes are:

r 0,	**zero offset**
r nn ,	**constant offset**
r A,	**accumulator A offset**
r B,	**accumulator B offset**
r D,	**accumulator D offset**
r ,+	**autoincrement by 1**
r ,++	**autoincrement by 2**
r ,-	**autodecrement by 1**
r ,--	**autodecrement by 2**
nn ,PCR	**constant offset from PC**

r is one of the registers X, Y, U, or S
nn is a twos-complement (signed) offset

All of the indexed modes except autoincrement/decrement by 1

also have an Indirect form. This is specified by appending the suffix [] after the addressing mode, e.g.:

r ,++ []	**indirect autoincrement by 2**

The TFR and EXG instructions take the form:

src dst TFR	**src dst EXG**

where src and dst can be any of the 16-bit registers D, X, Y, U, S, PC; or any of the 8-bit registers A, B, CCR, DPR.

Branch offsets for relative jumps are computed internally by the assembler; the operand for a relative jump is the destination address.

The following control structures are provided by the assembler:

cc IF, ... THEN
do code if cc satisfied

cc IF, ..1.. ELSE, ..2.. THEN,
do code ..1.. if cc satisfied, else do code ..2

BEGIN, ... cc UNTIL,
loop through code until cc satisfied;
always executes at least once

BEGIN, ..1.. cc WHILE, ..2.. REPEAT,
loop through code until cc satisfied;
exit is evaluated and taken after code ..1..
is executed (always at least once)

where the condition code cc is any of the following:

CC	**carry clear**	**LS lower or same**
CS	**carry set**	**LT less than**
EQ	**equal/zero**	**MI minus**
GE	**greater or equal**	**NE not equal/not zero**
GT	**greater**	**PL plus**
HI	**higher**	**ALW always**
HS	**higher or same**	**NVR never**
LE	**less than or equal**	**VC overflow clear**
LO	**lower**	**VS overflow set**

Infinite loops should use the 'NVR' (never true) condition code:

```
BEGIN, ... NVR UNTIL,
```

C. FIGURE ONE:

FORTH AND MOTOROLA ASSEMBLERS COMPARISON CHART

This chart shows the Forth assembler's equivalent for all of the Motorola assembler instructions and addressing modes.

This is not an exhaustive permutation of addressing modes and instructions; it is merely intended to illustrate the syntax for all possible addressing modes in each instruction group.

Refer to a 6809 data sheet for descriptions of allowable operands, operand ranges, and addressing modes for each instruction.

Instructions which require two operands (TFR and EXG) have the operands specified in the order: source, destination.
(This is only significant for the TFR instruction.)

INDEXED ADDRESSING MODES

```
                   -NON-INDIRECT--    ---INDIRECT----
TYPE             MOTOROLA  FORTH    MOTOROLA  FORTH     POSTBYTE

no offset          ,r       r 0,     [,r]      r 0, []   1rri0100
 5 bit offset     n,r       r n ,    defaults to 8-bit   0rrnnnnn
 8 bit offset     n,r       r n ,    [n,r]     r n , []  1rri1000
16 bit offset     n,r       r n ,    [n,r]     r n , []  1rri1001

A-reg offset      A,r       r A,     [A,r]     r A, []   1rri0110
B-reg offset      B,r       r B,     [B,r]     r B, []   1rri0101
D-reg offset      D,r       r D,     [D,r]     r D, []   1rri1011

incr. by 1         ,r+      r ,+       not allowed       1rr00000
incr. by 2         ,r++     r ,++    [,r++]    r ,++ []  1rri0001
decr. by 1         ,r-      r ,-       not allowed       1rr00010
decr. by 2         ,r--     r ,--    [,r--]    r ,-- []  1rri0011

PC ofs. 8 bit    n,PCR    n ,PCR   [n,PCR]   n ,PCR [] 1xxi1100
PC ofs. 16 bit   n,PCR    n ,PCR   [n,PCR]   n ,PCR [] 1xxi1101

16 bit address     not allowed      [n]       n []      10011111
```

where n = a signed integer value,
r = X (00), Y (01), U (10), or S (11)
x = don't care

INSTRUCTION SET

Inherent addressing group

MOTOROLA	FORTH		MOTOROLA	FORTH
ABX	ABX,		MUL	MUL,
ASLA	ASLA,		NEGA	NEGA,
ASLB	ASLB,		NEGB	NEGB,
ASRA	ASRA,		NOP	NOP,
ASRB	ASRB,		ORA	ORA,
CLRA	CLRA,		ORB	ORB,
CLRB	CLRB,		ROLA	ROLA,
COMA	COMA,		ROLB	ROLB,
COMB	COMB,		RORA	RORA,
DAA	DAA,		RORB	RORB,
DECA	DECA,		RTI	RTI,
DECB	DECB,		RTS	RTS,
INCA	INCA,		SEX	SEX,
INCB	INCB,		SWI	SWI,
LSLA	LSLA,		SWI2	SWI2,
LSLB	LSLB,		SWI3	SWI3,
LSRA	LSRA,		SYNC	SYNC,
LSRB	LSRB,		TSTA	TSTA,
			TSTB	TSTB,

Register-register group

MOTOROLA	FORTH		MOTOROLA	FORTH
EXG s,d	s d EXG		TFR s,d	s d TFR

Immediate-addressing-only group

MOTOROLA	FORTH		MOTOROLA	FORTH
ANDCC #n	n # ANDCC,		PSHS regs	n # PSHS,
CWAI #n	n # CWAI,		PSHU regs	n # PSHU,
ORCC #n	n # ORCC,		PULS regs	n # PULS,
			PULU regs	n # PULU,

Note:
Motorola allows the PSH and PUL instructions to contain a register list.
The Forth assembler requires the programmer to compute the bit mask for this list and supply it as an immediate argument.

Indexed-addressing-only group

(with example addressing modes)

MOTOROLA	FORTH		MOTOROLA	FORTH
LEAS D,U	U ,D LEAS,		LEAX [,S++]	S ,++ [] LEAX,
LEAU -5,Y	Y -5 , LEAU,		LEAY [1234]	1234 [] LEAY,

General-addressing group

(with example addressing modes)

MOTOROLA	FORTH		MOTOROLA	FORTH
ADCA #20	20 # ADCA,		LDA #20	20 # LDA,
ADCB <30	30 <> ADCB,		LDB <30	30 <> LDB,
ADDA 2000	2000 ADDA,		LDD 2000	2000 LDD,
ADDB [1030]	1030 [] ADDB,		LDS [1030]	1030 [] LDS,
ADDD ,S	S 0, ADDD,		LDU ,X	X 0, LDU,
ANDA 23,U	U 23 , ANDA,		LDX 23,Y	Y 23 , LDX,
ANDB A,X	X A, ANDB,		LDY A,S	S A, LDY,
ASL B,Y	Y B, ASL,		LSL B,U	U B, LSL,
ASR D,X	X D, ASR,		LSR D,S	S D, LSR,
BITA ,S+	S ,+ BITA,		NEG ,X+	X ,+ NEG,

BITB ,X++	X ,++ BITB,		ORA ,S++	S ,++ ORA,
CLR ,Y-	Y ,- CLR,		ORB ,U-	U ,- ORB,
CMPA ,U--	U ,-- CMPA,		ROL ,Y--	Y ,-- ROL,
CMPB -5,PCR	-5 ,PCR CMPB,		ROR 12,PCR	12 ,PCR ROR,
CMPD [,Y]	Y 0, [] CMPD,		SBCA [,U]	U 0, [] SBCA,
CMPS [7,Y]	Y 7 , [] CMPS,		SBCB [7,U]	U 7 , [] SBCB,
CMPU [A,S]	S A, [] CMPU,		STA [A,X]	X A, [] STA,
CMPX [B,U]	U B, [] CMPX,		STB [B,Y]	Y B, [] STB,
CMPY [D,X]	X D, [] CMPY,		STD [D,S]	S D, [] STD,
EORA [,Y+]	Y ,+ [] EORA,		STS [,U+]	U ,+ [] STS,
EORB [,U++]	U ,++ [] EORB,		STU [,Y++]	Y ,++ [] STU,
COM [,S-]	S ,- [] COM,		STX [,S-]	S ,- [] STX,
DEC [,X--]	X ,-- [] DEC,		STY [,X--]	X ,-- [] STY,
INC [5,PCR]	5 ,PCR [] INC,		SUBA [3,PCR]	3 ,PCR [] SUBA,
JMP [300]	300 [] JMP,		SUBB [300]	300 [] SUBB,
JSR 1234	1234 JSR,		SUBD 1234	1234 SUBD,
			TST #2	2 # TST,

Note that, in the Forth assembler, # signifies Immediate addressing, and <> signifies Direct addressing.

Many instructions do not allow immediate addressing.
Refer to the Motorola data sheet.

Branch instructions

MOTOROLA	FORTH		MOTOROLA	FORTH
BCC label	adrs BCC,		BLT label	adrs BLT,
BCS label	adrs BCS,		BMI label	adrs BMI,
BEQ label	adrs BEQ,		BNE label	adrs BNE,
BGE label	adrs BGE,		BPL label	adrs BPL,
BGT label	adrs BGT,		BRA label	adrs BRA,
BHI label	adrs BHI,		BRN label	adrs BRN,
BHS label	adrs BHS,		BSR label	adrs BSR,
BLE label	adrs BLE,		BVC label	adrs BVC,
BLO label	adrs BLO,		BVS label	adrs BVS,
BLS label	adrs BLS,			

The branch instructions in the Forth assembler expect an absolute address.

The relative offset is computed, and the "long branch" form of the instruction is used if necessary.

D. INTERNAL GLOSSARY AND DESCRIPTION

This assembler was written before I acquired the habit of "shadow screen" documentation. So, I'll document all of the unusual words and features here.
(Please refer to the program listing.)

The word WITHIN is a common Forth extension. The words 5BIT? and 8BIT? decide if a given value will fit in a 5-bit or 8-bit signed integer, so we can choose the correct indexed addressing mode.

The synonym (,) is defined because later I redefine, as an addressing mode.

ALIGN etc. deserve some comment.

This assembler was originally written for a metacompiler running on a 68000 system, which insisted upon word-aligning the DP after each Forth word was interpreted. This meant that any 6809 instruction which assembled an odd number of bytes would have a filler byte added -- with catastrophic results!

I fixed this by causing all of the assembler words to do the aligning themselves. Thus, the 68000 Forth never inserted any filler, and I always knew when the DP had been adjusted.
HERE and **C,** were redefined accordingly.

The word W, allows 6809 word operands to be compiled on either big-endian or little-endian host machines.
>< is a byte-swap operator provided by the Forth I used.

Some 6809 instructions have a one-byte opcode, and some have two bytes.
Opcodes are stored as a 16-bit value.
If the high 8 bits are nonzero, they are the first opcode byte.
OPCODE, lays down one or two bytes, accordingly.

The MODE variable indicates whether the addressing mode is Immediate, Direct, Indexed, or Extended. # and <> set the first two modes; Extended is the default when no mode is set. (This is the first addressing-mode technique described in the previous article.)

The Indexed addressing modes in the 6809 add a "postbyte" to the opcode, which contains mode information and a register number (for X, Y, U, or S).
INDEXREG puts the two-bit register number into the postbyte, and also sets MODE.

Note that the postbyte is passed on the stack.
(This is the second addressing-mode technique.)

XMODE defines the "simple" Indexed modes.
These modes each have a fixed postbyte, modified only by the register number (as supplied by INDEXREG).
For example, the word ,++ fetches the postbyte 81 hex and then invokes INDEXREG to insert the two register bits.

The word , rearranges the stack and builds the postbyte for the constant-offset Indexed mode.

The word ,PCR provides the postbyte for the PC-relative Indexed mode. Since this has no register operand, INDEXREG isn't used.
MODE must be explicitly set to 20 hex.

The word [] indicates indirection.
For the Indexed addressing modes, this is done by setting the "indirect" bit in the postbyte.
(This is an example of the third addressing-mode technique.)
For the Direct addressing mode, [] must change the mode to Indexed and supply the Extended Indirect postbyte.

Register definitions are simple CONSTANTs.
Note that the synonyms W, IP, RP, and SP are defined for the registers X, Y, S, and U.
I use these synonyms when writing Forth kernels.

INHOP defines the Inherent (no operands) instructions.

IMMOP defines the Immediate-only instructions. These all expect a byte operand, and they check to make sure that the # addressing mode was specified (MODE=0).

RROP defines the register-register instructions, TFR and EXG. Note that it doesn't check that both operands are the same size; the programmer is presumed to know better.

+MODE is a fudge. All of the general-addressing instructions form their opcodes by adding 0, 10, 20, or 30 hex to a base value, EXCEPT those instructions whose Direct opcode takes the form 0x hex.
These instructions use 6x for Indexed mode, and 7x for Extended, so the assembler assumes a "base opcode" of 4x, and adds 10, 20, or 30 hex.
(There is no Immediate mode for these instructions.)

Then, if the resulting opcode is 5x, we know that Direct mode was specified, and the opcode should really be 0x hex. +MODE applies the MODE value to the base opcode; it then checks for 5x opcodes and changes them to 0x.

PCREL lays the postbyte and operand for PC-relative addressing. If the signed offset fits in 8 bits, the postbyte is modified for the short form and a single-byte operand is used. Otherwise, the long form postbyte and two-byte operand is used.

NOTINDIR? checks the indirection bit in the postbyte.

COFSET lays the postbyte and operand for constant-offset Indexed addressing.
If the offset fits in 5 bits, and indirection is not used, then the postbyte is modified for the 5-bit offset.
Otherwise, if the offset fits in 8 bits, the postbyte is modified for the 8-bit form (single-byte operand);
if the offset requires 16 bits, the long form is used (two-byte operand).

EXTIND lays the postbyte and operand for Extended Indirect addressing.

INDEXED lays the postbyte and (if required) operand for all of the Indexed modes. COFSET, PCREL, and EXTIND are the special cases which require operands; a CASE statement identifies these by the postbyte value.
All other postbyte values are "simple" modes which have no operands; they are handled in the default clause of the CASE statement.

Some 6809 Immediate instructions require an 8-bit operand, and some a 16-bit operand. Others don't allow Immediate mode.

IMMED handles this by testing the second parmeter in an opcode word defined by GENOP, and laying one or two operand bytes, accordingly.
If "zero" operand bytes are indicated, this means that this addressing mode is invalid with this instruction.

GENOP defines the instructions which can have any addressing mode. It selects one of four actions depending on MODE. As noted above, the parameter "immedsize" can be used to disallow Immediate mode for any instruction.

INXOP defines the instructions which can have Indexed addressing mode. It checks that the MODE value is correct (20 hex) before assembling the instruction.

CONDBR and **UNCBR** build the branch instructions. They are identical, except in how they modify the instruction when the long form is required. CONDBR makes the long form by prefixing a 10 hex byte; UNCBR makes the long form by substituting an alternate opcode (both opcodes are stored in a 16-bit value).
Both of these words take an absolute address, and compute the relative offset from the branch instruction; the short or long form of the branch is then automatically chosen.

CS through **NVR** are condition code CONSTANTs for the structured conditionals. These are actually the opcodes which must be assembled by the conditionals such as IF, and UNTIL, .
As noted in the previous article, IF, and UNTIL, must actually assemble the logical inverse of the stated condition; this is handled in the 6809 assembler by defining each of these constants to contain the "inverse" opcode.
For example, the constant CS (carry set) actually contains the opcode for a BCC instruction. This is because the phrase CS IF, must assemble a BCC.

Structured conditionals were described in detail in the previous article.
Since the condition codes are in fact opcodes, the requisite conditional jumps can be assembled directly with C, .
Also, these conditionals use the fig-Forth "compiler security": each conditional leaves a constant value on the stack, which much be verified (by ?PAIRS) by its matching word.
For example, IF, leaves 2 on the stack; ELSE, and ENDIF, (a.k.a. THEN,) do a 2 ?PAIRS to resolve this.

ENTERCODE CODE and **;CODE** are, of necessity, "tuned" to a particular Forth implementation.
For example, since this fig-Forth model's CREATE automatically sets up the code field properly, it's not necessary for CODE to patch the code field to point to the new machine code.
Other Forth models have a different assumption, so some phrase such as CREATE HERE 2- ! will no doubt be needed to set the code field pointer.

ENTERCODE (and thus CODE and ;CODE) also use !CSP to check for stack imbalances.
This means that each CODE definition must end with ;C
(which uses ?CSP to resolve !CSP).

;C also unSMUDGEs the Forth word being defined. These are also fig-Forth usages, which may not apply to your Forth model.

Finally, **NEXT,** is an example of a simple assembler macro.
It assembles the two-instruction sequence which is the inner interpreter (NEXT) of an indirect-threaded 6809 Forth. NEXT is a synonym.

Publications by Bradford J. Rodriguez

updated 18 Apr 2014 (added Forth Multitasking in a Nutshell)
NOTE REGARDING LINKS: *Regarding all links in this Book, we have no control if they are still available – and sorry, if they are not.*

A selection of papers I have published, seminars I have presented, and computer programs I have written, that are available on this site. Please note that many of the papers include illustrations -- your browser should support GIF files. Detailed drawings are sometimes offered as **PDF** (Adobe Acrobat) files.

Moving Forth: a series on writing Forth kernels

This series originally appeared in The Computer Journal. Accompanying source code can be found on the CamelForth page.

- Part 1: Design Decisions in the Forth Kernel (33K text, 21K images)
- Part 2: Benchmarks and Case Studies of Forth Kernels (31K text)
- Part 3: Demystifying DOES> (48K text, 45K images)
- Part 4: Assemble or Metacompile? (8K text)
- Part 5: The Z80 Primitives (9K text, 38K linked files)
- Part 6: The Z80 High-level Kernel (20K text, 36K linked files)
- Part 7: CamelForth for the 8051 (12K text, 5K images)
- Part 8: CamelForth for the 6809 (10K text, 33K linked files)
- Multitasking 8051 CamelForth (23K **PDF** file)

Multiprocessing for the Impoverished: a multi-6809 system

This series originally appeared in The Computer Journal.

- Part 1: A 6809 Uniprocessor (28K text, 37K linked **PDF** files)
- Part 2: Sharing the Bus (18K text, 44K images)
- Part 3: Mid-Course Corrections (21K text, 156K linked **PDF** file)
- Part 4: The IBM PC Bus (21K text, 156K linked **PDF** file)
- Part 5: Serial I/O (34K text, 163K linked **PDF** files)

An Embedded Temporal Expert For Control of a Tandem Accelerator

My 1997 Ph.D. dissertation at McMaster University.

Summary articles.

- A System for Distributed Inferencing (with W.F.S. Poehlman) [1996 Rochester Forth Conference] (24K text, 77K linked files)

Full text of dissertation.

These are all **PDF** files and require Adobe's Acrobat Reader.

- Front matter (abstract, acknowledgments, table of contents, list of figures; 20K)
- Chapter 1: Introduction (17K)
- Chapter 2: Literature Review (40K)
- Chapter 3: An Embedded Temporal Expert System (43K)
- Chapter 4: Controlling the FN Accelerator (85K)
- Chapter 5: Expert System Performance (26K)
- Chapter 6: Accelerator Control Performance (259K)
- Chapter 7: Summary and Conclusions (9K)
- Bibliography (35K)
- Appendix A: Instrumenting the FN Accelerator (140K)
- Appendix B: Asynchronous Token Ring Communications (35K)
- Appendix C: Toward a Distributed, Object-Based Forth (29K)
- Appendix D: The Inferencing Token Language (9K)
- Appendix E: Accelerator Control Program (13K)
- Appendix F: Towers of Hanoi Benchmark (11K)
- Appendix G: Glossary of Abbreviations (4K)

PatternForth: A Pattern-Matching Language for Real-Time Control

My 1989 M.S. dissertation at Bradley University.

Full text of dissertation.

These are HTML files with GIF images.

- A. Introduction (7K)
- B. Project Scope (8K)
- C. Dynamic Memory Management (19K, 15K linked images)
- D. Associative String Access (39K, 26K linked images)
- E. Pattern Matching (44K, 64K linked images)
- F. Pattern and String Operations (14K)
- G. Conclusions (1K)
- H. References (6K)

- I. Figures (2K, 105K linked images)
- Appendix A. PatternForth Glossary (21K)
- Appendix B. The Program Listing *(pending)*

Miscellaneous Papers

- Forth Multitasking in a Nutshell [from The Computer Journal #58] (50K text) NEW
- Asynchronous Serial I/O With The PSC1000 [1998 FORML conference] (29K text, 9K images), and program listing.
- The "Ztar" MIDI Controller [1998 FORML conference] (12K text, 101K image)
- Object Oriented Forth and Building Automation Control[1998 FORML conference] (24K text)
- A Survey of Object-Oriented Forths (with W.F.S. Poehlman) [from ACM SIGPLAN Notices 31:4] (17K text, 45K images)
- A Minimal TTL Processor for Architecture Exploration[1994 ACM Symposium on Applied Computing] (17K text, 22K images, 93K linked **PDF** file)
- The Echelon Lighting Control System [1992 Rochester Forth Conference] (27K text, 25K images)
- A BNF Parser in Forth [from ACM SIGForth Newsletter 2:2] (27K text)
- Build Your Own (Cross-) Assembler...in Forth[from The Computer Journal #52] (33K text)
- Build Your Own Assembler, Part 2: a 6809 Forth Assembler[from The Computer Journal #54] (21K text)
- 6809 Forth Assembler Listing [from The Computer Journal #54] (11K text)

  You can also see the master index of everything I have written, on or off the web.

Computer Programs

- CamelForth for the 6809, with Chromium metacompiler
- CamelForth for the 8051, w/multitasker
- CamelForth for the Z80 under CP/M
- CamelForth for the 8086 under MS-DOS

Bradford J. Rodriguez | CamelForth | T-Recursive Technology | Send us email

####

Appendix:

Some related Links

http://www.bradrodriguez.com/

http://www.bradrodriguez.com/resume.htm

http://www.bradrodriguez.com/papers/

http://www.bradrodriguez.com/papers/mindex.html

http://www.camelforth.com/news.php?default.0.30

https://github.com/DRuffer/coinForth/blob/master/amforth-5.8/doc/htdocs/TG/recipes/1wire.html

http://amforth.sourceforge.net/TG/recipes/1wire.html

https://radaris.com/p/Brad/Rodriguez/

Some Pictures re-drawn

A short note from Juergen Pintaske:

In addition to just reformatting and publishing this material, I wanted to understand the pictures as much as possible, and as well how all of these addess lists hang together.

As it turned out, grasping it and to redraw the pictures will take more time than planned.

There was a decision that had to be taken:
    Publish like the original material now
    or
    Delay the publication
    and include the additional material.
As this was an eBook first, and is planned for educational purposes,
and more material might be added anyway, I decided:
Time to get it out.

Material will be added as part of the update process.
And then with the link to a place where parts can be downloaded.
Here just one picture, showing address areas of the dictionary to be filled as you read the eBook. Here starting from boundaries, but could start anywhere and with variable length.

0	1	2	3	4	5	6	7	8	9	A	B	C	D	E	F

ADDRESS	0	1	2	3	4	5	6	7	8	9	A	B	C	D	E	F
CELL																

ADDRESS	0	1	2	3	4	5	6	7	8	9	A	B	C	D	E	F
CELL																

ADDRESS	0	1	2	3	4	5	6	7	8	9	A	B	C	D	E	F
CELL																

These eBooks are a spare time activity - and job, family, dog come first. So it might take time
Juergen Pintaske – Exmark - April 2018

Bradford J. Rodriguez, Ph.D.

Embedded and Distributed Control Systems -- contract design and development of microprocessor hardware and software, for maximum performance on limited resources in HW and SW.

SELECTED PROJECTS see it all at http://www.bradrodriguez.com/resume.htm	
2013	**ALN11 Controller:** Created a single-board ARM replacing discontinued 8051 board. New board uses Philips LPC2138 (ARM7 family);
2013	**Wireless Anemometer:** Wrote in GCC for a micropower 915 MHz wireless anemometer, MSP430G2553 MCU, and the TI CC1150 SPI transmitter, operates on accumulated wind energy.
2011	**DT12 Controller:** Designed a single-board computer as drop-in replacement for OEM board, for a low-power battery operated test instrument, from 6303 PolyForth to MC9S12X SwiftX Forth.
2011-present	**MiniPods:** Developed software for a family of 2.4 GHz devices to log work hours, travel distance, fuel dispensing, and operator inspections. Implemented in Forth using MC9S12, MC13202 transceiver.
2009-2011	**USB OSBDM Linux drivers:** Software to control an Open Source BDM device from a Linux desktop via USB. OSBDM, debug for 9S08, 9S12, and 9S12X microcontrollers.
2006-present	**D6 ZPC:** Ongoing development and maintenance of the "ZPC" software on the "D6" hardware, in Forth and H8 assembler. New and improved features include expanded and multitrack MIDI recording.
2008	**MSP430 CamelForth:** Developed a Forth compiler/interpreter for the Texas Instruments MSP430 processor; less than 6K bytes of ROM, and offers "direct-to-Flash" compilation
2006-2007	**SuperPod:** Converted the IsoPod operating software for this new board using the Freescale DSP56F8365 processor. The core was converted from C to assembler for threefold greater speed.
1994	**CamelForth:** Developed CamelForth, a portable ANS Forth compiler for Harvard and von Neumann processors, with implementations for Z80, 8051, and 6809.
1993	**68HC16 MPE Forth:** Wrote MPE Forth for the 68HC16: Kernel, multitasker, and documentation.
1991	**Z8 MPE Forth:** Wrote MPE Forth for Z8/Super8, including kernel, multitasker, and documentation.
1987	**VectorForth:** Developed software for PC-based array processing workstation. Wrote assembler and system interface for Vortex and Point-I array coprocessor boards, polyForth language support.
1978-present	Personal research: Forth kernels, expert systems, assemblers, metacompiler and A "Minimal" Microprogrammed Forth Machine using Standard TTL

EDUCATION	
1998	Ph.D. in Electrical Engineering, McMaster University,
1989	M.S. in Computer Science, Bradley University.
1980	M.S. in Electrical Engineering, Bradley University.
1977	B.S. in Electrical Engineering, Bradley University.

MISCELLANEOUS

Languages: Fluent in Forth, C, and assembler for 6502, 6809, 68HC11, 68HC12, 68HC16, 68000, 8051, 8080, 8086, ARM7, H8/S, LSI-11, MSP430, Super8, Z8, Z80. Proficient in Pascal, BASIC, FORTRAN, PHP, Tcl.

Operating Systems: Experienced with Unix, Linux, RT-11, CP/M, MS/DOS, polyFORTH, FreeRTOS.

Exmark published v15 – 11 August 2018

www.ingramcontent.com/pod-product-compliance
Lightning Source LLC
Chambersburg PA
CBHW031548080326
40690CB00054B/737

* 9 7 8 1 7 1 8 1 2 4 9 9 8 *